ground & be free

A PRACTICAL GUIDE TO RELEASE
EMOTIONAL PAIN & ENJOY SOVEREIGNTY

Grounding is the single most supportive and
transformative process to have in your toolbox.
Applying it in all areas of your life is the easiest way
to regain control over your emotional freedom.

MERINA B ELDAN

Designed by Merina B Eldan
Editing support by Mistilei Wriston
campgroundtbd@gmail.com
All visual art-work is copyright Merina B Eldan.

FIRST EDITION

This guide is intended as a reference volume only, not as a medical manual. By reading this book you agree that the author of this book takes no responsibility for any reactions you may or may not have by performing the meditations and exercises described herein. This book is not intended as a substitute for the medical advice of a physician.

ISBN: 979-8-9904910-2-1

With gratitude to my lineage:

My grandmothers, and my great grandmothers, the keepers of the knowledge, plant wisdom, clear seeing and Spiritual Medicine. Thank you for preserving and honing your abilities despite the times of persecution and disregard for your wisdom. Thank you for continuing to teach me your ways through the Divine Ākāśa.

With gratitude to my teachers:

From my early days of living in an ashram in India, to the zoom calls during the pandemic, my teachers held a sacred container through which I was able to liberate myself from pain and reconnect to my true Self. Indradyumna Swami, Niranjan Swami, Jeffrey Armstrong | Kavindra Rishi, Tony Robbins, Joe Dispenza, Amir Khalighi, Rev. Lisa French, Eva Clay, Christopher Witecki, Cody Edner, you have made the biggest impact on my growth as a human and a soul. Thank you.

Special gratitude to Lewis for transmitting teachings from the Ākāśa. Thank you for gifting us with a curriculum that provides the tools to gain control of our 7th chakra and to claim ultimate freedom as a spirit in a body.

With gratitude to my community:

This guide is also dedicated to the MAHALO.care community and supporters filled with beautiful, awe-inspiring humans.

Preface

I am a modern woman, mystic, entrepreneur, master skin care formulator, lady of adventure, and a lineage holder of clairvoyant Spiritual Medicine. My extra-sense, psychic and mediumship abilities were passed down through my family generation, and honed-in with professional training allowing me to transmit the Universal Wisdom from the Divine Ākāśa.

I am thankful to know my gifts. One is helping people know how beautiful they are, from my global beauty brand, MAHALO Skin Care, to the Conscious Grounding practice I will introduce in this guide. I have searched the world to study with the most scholarly and spiritual teachers and found my connection to my freedom and my sovereignty right under my feet.

There are so many important and dividing topics in our world and so many trying to influence us. I take great comfort in knowing I have a tool to use at any moment to get stable, clear, calm, and ultimately free to be. A grounded human is a beautiful human, and I am honored to share this with you.

What you seek is seeking you ~ *Rumi*

Beauty will save the world ~ *Dostoevsky*

Freedom is the oxygen of the soul

At first glance, these three quotes might not have an apparent correlation. All three have had the misfortune of becoming cliche, found anywhere from bumper stickers to Instagram posts. Idealistic, inspiring, and also somewhat distant. Still, they hold a resonance that tugs on a cord of hope. At least, I hope they do so for you. This book is a guide, toolkit, and exploratory journey leading you to claim your innate capacities for hope, connection, creativity, authenticity, sensitivity, resourcefulness, inner peace, success, freedom, happiness, well-being, intuition, beauty, and ultimate freedom.

These states and capacities are a part of every one of us. No dogma, school of thought, physical product, religious or even spiritual system is required to embody them. True authentic "being-ness" does not belong to an organization or framework. The expression of authentic self, a state of freedom, is the universal message of all teachers and holy people, best summed up by Rumi: "What you seek is seeking you."

Why does something so intrinsically "us" feel distant and hard to reach? If beauty is an innate part of who we are, part of the ancient trinity of Truth, Goodness, and Beauty, and if "freedom is the oxygen of the soul," why do we often feel jailed by our circumstances? Why does the search for beauty often feel like pain and disappointment? Why is there so much confusion in the human experience?

In this guide, I explore how we can gain authentic control and claim our individual freedom. This personal practice requires a desire to be free from pain, re-engaging the creative part of your brain, and a child-like attitude of play to reconnect with ourselves.

A child-like attitude is an important part of this process and might feel like effort to some. Many of us have been raised in a society conditioned by seriousness and the "do the work" approach to self-work, including traditional routes of counseling, talk therapy, or more esoteric practices of meditation and healing. The "no pain, no gain" attitude is hard to shake off. Let that be okay.

We will explore the shifts in perspective that can allow us to approach this "work" as play. In essence, this work truly is play. It is not serious in the way brain surgery is. It is by no means as complicated as understanding "The Ulysses" might be. This process truly is rather simple, so simple that many will be astounded by how something so playfully easy can deliver a palpable sense of inner freedom, joy, beauty, and all the spectrum of emotional states.

This simple process can also prepare and guide us to face some of the difficult emotional states of anger, anxiety, unworthiness, lack, defeat, and so forth. We can face and acknowledge them or just release them, creating space for the ultimate freedom from pain so we can claim more of whatever we truly want.

Merina B Eldan
March 2024
Kaua'i, Hawai'i

Introduction

Eliminating Human Suffering

Ancient and neo-spiritual traditions, religions, energy practices, therapies, and the various forms of healing or inquiry have a shared blueprint of seeking to find and deliver a way of eliminating human suffering. Like many, I explored a range of systems and ways that expand my awareness, encompassing clinical psychology, somatic practices, nutrition, and brain chemistry to holistic modalities like beauty practices, metaphysics, energy techniques, breathing, spiritual traditions, chanting, and others. In all these explorations, conscious Grounding and releasing pain were of considerable practical advantage. My experience and practice sessions with clients created a measurable impact and inspired the writing of this guide.

Effortless Practice

Contrary to the emotionally rich elements of other practices, Grounding and releasing is pragmatic and effortless. There are countless examples, including personal applications, where the efficacy of this process produces measurable results in creating positive changes and reducing emotional and physiologic responses to stress.

Grounding is a matter-of-fact, unbiased technique for freeing oneself from pain, emotional blockages, attachments, repetitive thought patterns, negative self-talk, unworthiness, resentment, etc. Conscious engagement with this non-denominational, nonsecular practice, not belonging to anything or anyone, allows you to free yourself from pain. Indirectly, it plays homage to a Buddhist saying that attachment is the primary cause of suffering. By releasing your pain, you are releasing your emotional attachments.

Finding Your Way to Freedom

We Are Being Manipulated

On the flip side of spiritual, religious, and philosophical traditions, is an often overlooked modern aspect that permeates all areas of our lives: *marketing*. Marketing is a gigantic machine centered on the promise to relieve us from suffering, solve our problems, make us beautiful, and provide pleasure. It does so on the premise of assuring that relief from our pain is literally just around the corner. Just one more purchase, and you'll be free from pain.

Marketing in the beauty world, an industry I have been involved in for over 15 years, is a great example.

Advertisements from the 1900s are rarely much different from those in the 2020s. Buying this cream and the latest technology fades your wrinkles. It makes you feel beautiful, freeing you from pain and providing happiness, community, connection, acceptance, love, and worthiness.

The same marketing blueprint applies to almost anything: cars, toothpaste, hamburgers, vacations, and insurance policies. The core reason why we respond over and over to the tugs of their cues is our need to be free of pain. Whether the marketed product or service answers a desire, solves a problem, or provides something, the blueprint of that structure operates on and pushes on our pain. Like it or not, we are being manipulated.

Journey of the Search

Like many, you may have begun your journey and exploration. Some have worked with experts with Ivy League degrees, and spent hours laying on leather couches talking through feelings, dissecting every element of how the narcissistic mother or father traumatized and wounded them. I remember calling on my inner child, embracing myself tightly while crying and repeating aloud: I love you, I am here for you, I matter. And still, I knew there was more inside me, inside each of us.

I took massive action and signed up for week-long self-development boot camps, spending 12+ hours a day stepping into massive potential. I have meditated, integrated, breathed in, and breathed out with mouth closed or open. I grew from these and yet never felt complete.

Some of us took it further on the path of finding the answer. Surely, an Amazonian shaman could show us the way to freedom from pain. Some drank the ancient root tea, hugged trees, spoke with clouds, sang tribal chants, and sweated in lodges. Some communed with spirit guides, traveled to India, Thailand, or Bali, and maybe became vegetarian, vegan, Keto, or Raw. Did you drink celery juice, fast and switch to alkaline water?

They all helped. They all taught me something. They all worked as tools in my development toolkit until I found the most fun, powerful and easy tool, Conscious Grounding.

Oh, Human!

Well, this list isn't made to be a lighthearted poke at you or me. If any, some, or all of these have resonated and have been a part of your journey as a human, Hi, me too! Acknowledge your determination to keep searching and believe that the answer to our desire for freedom, to be free from pain, is just around the corner. There is an inner drive that propels us forward. Even if, at times, be they minutes, weeks, or years when we might stumble, lose hope, get disillusioned, or depressed, we eventually get up and press on, wondering where we haven't searched, what we haven't done enough of, or too much.

If you are like I was, maybe you felt you needed to try harder. Or maybe you felt the "solution" simply doesn't exist.

Where Are You in Your Search?

Where are you on the map of this journey? Have you just begun the exploration? Are you halfway through transitioning from micro-dosing psilocybin to considering hypnosis? Are you reading this guide on the way to a retreat in Peru? Are you in a place where you feel that those parabens in your laundry detergent might not be as bad as you were told and will probably not solve the inner humming of pain you have been so masterfully numbing or avoiding using sulfate-free shampoo?

Or are you in a space where you are just confused? That bottle of Jasmine Rose spray didn't bring you the happiness promised by the marketer, or that past life regression workshop left you even more confused about what to do with your present life. Maybe you resonated with the practices you have embarked on, and now your reality has shifted so much that you can't grasp or are consciously ready for the next step.

Do You Want To Be in Control?

Whatever stage you are in, from the Universe's perspective, you are exactly where you need to be. The only question to ask here is: Do you want to be in control of your freedom and pain?

The Way to Enlightenment

In Buddhism, one of the highest states of awareness and self-realization is when one can look compassionately at a man beating the dog and the dog itself. Reaching that level of inner liberation, freedom, and enlightenment is difficult, especially when attempted with seriousness through dogma, discipline, and rigorous practice. But even if one does attain that state through those means of effort, the ego swoops in, wrapping one up in pride of possessing the answer. You may momentarily feel like you have THE answer! But do you?

Finding a New Perspective Through Humor

There is another perspective through which one may seek awareness and self-realization—play. It is much more manageable to look at layers of human conditioning through the lens of amusement and even better through the child-like perspective of play. *Enlightened, not enlightened. Why does a bird sing or a dog bark? Can a cat moo?* - the child asks. In that child-like approach, there is ease. There is space and wonder. There is permission to be whatever, and however you are in the moment. That is your salvation. That play, that openness, that anything and everything is possible attitude is your best defense against the marketers and the gurus who are here to provide you with what they know you need. If you can be in a child-like perspective of play, this guide is for you.

An Exploratory Journey to Freedom

This book is both a guide, a toolkit, and an exploratory journey that will lead you to gain clarity and authentic control over your freedom, transcending your challenges along the way. The destination is not to provide you with answers but to liberate yourself from the pain from which those challenges originate.

There are no mantras to remember or lengthy protocols to follow. Each step is your own to create, visualize, and monitor. It "works" when you "work it," and it "works" better when you play with it. You witness the process you are actively engaged in on your own accord, so you can not be misled or manipulated here. The fun in this process is that it works for the enlightened, the cynic, the spiritualist, the academic, the atheist, the religionist, and the normalist. As long as you have a body, it will work for you.

Freedom is the oxygen of the soul, and what you are doing is creating more space to breathe it in fully.

The simplicity of this process allows you to utilize it anytime, anywhere. By actively and playfully re-activating the connection with the Earth and simply allowing gravity to take away the pain, you are creating a more significant capacity in your space to hold more happiness, experience real love, do things with less effort, and be overall healthier and blissful.

You Liberate Yourself

With time—and that length of time entirely depends on you —you will see a noticeable difference in yourself. You will become more solid and less bothered by things that used to trigger you or set you off. Thanksgiving dinners with the in-laws are a lot more smooth. Those poking political questions go right over your head, leaving you centered and whole. The "highs" you have experienced in some of the previous self-discovery workshops are no longer fleeting. You are more complete, authentically whole, and balanced. Whatever you do becomes more enjoyable, pleasurable, and nourishing.

Your skin care rituals reach a deeper level of self-care, where you meet the Divine beauty within yourself over and over: "Beauty will save the world."

Eventually, playing with the Earth's gravity to free yourself from pain will become a part of you. As you release pain and blockages, you will create more and more space to discover your inner Self. With more space to be yourself, you will begin to find your own answers to the questions you previously sought from external sources. In this moment, which will happen over and over, "What you seek is seeking you" will complete the circle of you, meeting you.

Be Amused

This guide is written as a storytelling journey, with you, the reader, in mind. It is simple, kindergarten simple, effortless, and playful. Be amused as you shift through the pages, and let the energy flowing through these words ease and calm you. Whether you flip through these pages, read it once, or return to it again, you will feel lighter, and things around you will feel more enjoyable. You are on a journey of freedom, and on this path, things get better and better.

Be Skeptical

It's okay to be skeptical, too. Many of us have explored various paths of seeking knowledge and answers and have been down the primrose path. So, be as skeptical as you like. It may serve you better than gushing enthusiasm, an inevitable setup for a letdown. Therefore, rather than enthusiasm, a curious observation will serve you better.

This journey shows how it feels to claim authentic freedom for yourself and how to do it without relying on others. Your mind will find amusement and enjoy information in the following stories and anecdotes. By engaging your mind, you will effortlessly activate the process of Grounding your pain, for it is the nature of the mind to seek relief from pain and suffering and to experience greater happiness.

Kindergarten

For some, reminiscing about childhood brings back memories of the boundless freedom and wonder that defined that time. Wasn't it fun? If your childhood experience wasn't quite as joyful, you now have another chance to give it a fun go. The word "kindergarten" originated in Germany and translates to "child's garden," a nurturing place where each person who enters is given an opportunity to thrive. Educational systems create kindergartens to help children discover the joys of making new friends and learning together, paving the way for future years of successful schooling ahead.

At its core, the pure essence of kindergarten embodies qualities of playfulness, acceptance, curiosity, openness to possibilities, and effortlessness. Even seriousness takes on a lighthearted tone when viewed through the lens of kindergarten. Perfectionism and the pressure to do things right are absent at this stage. Instead, there's an innate freedom to embrace things as they are, with neutrality and genuine curiosity.

The kindergarten level has a transfiguring effect.

Garden of Wonder

What does garden mean to you? Is it a place of beauty, growth, nourishment, and peace, a place to process, breathe, celebrate, discover, explore, and be in wonder? Perhaps it is a place for a bit of pruning, pulling weeds, healing wounds, and planting dreams. Maybe it's a place to pick fruits, eat juicy berries, or have a tea party under the wisteria vine. A garden can be all these things and more. A child's garden is where we can find our soul's roots and rediscover, resurrect, and grow our dreams and ourselves into fruition. It is a safe sanctuary to explore, know and learn.

In this Garden of Wander, in this childlike state of wonder, people of all levels are welcomed and encouraged to grow here. In kindergarten, there's a sense of innocence and purity. It's a space where everyone is accepted just as they are. We can express ourselves however we like – whether new, advanced, silly, serious, joyful, sad, passionate, or even melancholic.

Kindergarten embodies a (play)ground of permission, where there are no limits on who we can be. It's a place where we can grow inner acceptance of ourselves exactly for who and where we are. With this acceptance comes more freedom to simply be ourselves. And when we embrace this freedom and relax into ourselves, that's when the real fun begins.

Where You Are is Okay

Being on the kindergarten level means accepting that where you are at this moment is okay. This permission to accept yourself can be of immense relief. Where you are right now is entirely okay. Why? Because it's where you are, your journey can only progress from now on. If we resist or struggle with accepting our current situation, it's like being trapped in quicksand – we become stuck and unable to move, and it's not fun at all. It's crucial to acknowledge where we are before we can confidently and safely take each new step forward.

In kindergarten: if you are feeling great or not so great, positive or not so positive, it's okay. If you are worried or fearful or happy and creative, it's OK. All you need to do is be you at this moment in time. If you're not sure what that is right now, don't worry. This is where the Grounding process comes into play to help you get into the moment and clear your path of obstacles. This process helps sweep away what is not you and discover what is you.

Kindergarten has nothing to do with being new, intermediate, or advanced. We come from different backgrounds and different levels of education. In this energy, each person is welcome exactly where they are. That includes how much you know or don't know about the Spiritual arena or anything else. It means where you are in your life right now, the kind of mood or energetic space you are in, is okay. Play is a state of being in which all who choose can learn to live. It allows us each a chance to be happy and free of competition, struggle, and pain. Let's play!

A Transfiguring Effect

Kindergarten can present challenges to some people. When you have stepped into the level of child-like wonder, you may appear threatening to others, as your authentic openness and full acceptance of self highlight the edges of *pain confetti* in others. Some people might feel you want something from them or that your freedom threatens their existence. They would be right to think that, in some way. The freedom of kindergarten threatens the existence of the *pain confetti* that has become a part of some people's identity.

Kindergarten is a state of being that transforms everything around you because it radiates that energy of openness, acceptance, freedom, and play. It happens on its own, and we don't have to "do" anything but just be in play.

The kindergarten, playful, curious level creates the container in which we can heal our bodies. It is an important part of the process shared in this guide.

Amusement

In kindergarten, in addition to play, openness, and wonder, there is another energy level, a tone of "amusement," or simply a sense of humor. One might consider that there's already quite enough seriousness on this planet!

Here, we're learning to let go of seriousness because it is a frozen vibration. When we do, we begin to lighten our vibration. As we lighten our energy, we can access freedom.

To that extent, an arsenal of "dad jokes" or funny short stories is often shared in personal practice, groups, and beauty and ritual sessions. For example, *"What do you call a fish wearing a bowtie? [Sophisticated]"*, or *"Have you heard about the chocolate record player? [It sounds pretty sweet]"*… Okay, one more: *"I asked my dog what's two minus two. [She said nothing.]"* These bring everyone an amusing chuckle and bring everyone to the kindergarten level.

Throughout this guide, you will see me using words and references from the level of Kindergarten and amusement. I use words and expressions like *"pain confetti"* when referring to traumatic pain and triggers or *"floating in a lava lamp"* to describe emotions. They are intended to continuously invite you to approach this information from the perspective of child-like wonder and play.

The Mind

One of the core principles to grasp is that the body obeys the mind and that the mind is the manifestation tool by which awareness and cognition take form. This principle is derived from the law of consciousness, which asserts that we are solely subject to the contents of our minds. The only influence or power anything holds over us is the belief we grant it. By "power," I mean the energy and determination to believe.

It is easy to be confused about the reliance on one's mind when freeing oneself from emotional attachments. We often seek answers from external sources, which can range from the mind being your worst enemy to the mind being the source of absolute logical truth.

Some spiritual and philosophical traditions offer compelling arguments against befriending your mind. They teach the mind is the "bad" ego; it leads us astray from truth. Countless meditation practices attempt to silence your mind or detach from your thinking. The in-between approach is also laden with theories and applications.

Mind as a Neutral Machine

We will approach the mind from a neutral angle, seeing it as a machine producing electrical currents that process and fuel various elements of our physical and mental bodies. It has a job and an expert-level capacity to generate powerful thoughts, create technologies that put humans on the Moon, speak languages, and, yes, communicate with our hearts (more on that later)—heating and cooling, clotting blood, experiencing fear, analyzing, and protecting, among other jobs. *Where attention goes, energy flows* is operated by the mind.

Thoughts and Feelings

The mind is an engine that, with its thoughts, is fueled by feelings. Each feeling is the progressive derivative of thousands of thoughts. Within each thought is either a repeated or newly created energy that holds various charges that repeat or attract another thought.

Throughout our lives, we numb, repress, disassociate, and try to escape from our feelings, creating an accumulation of suppressed energy. Imagine these suppressed energies as dots of confetti floating around the mind, bumping into each other, creating triggers and explosions.

The Floating Confetti of Pain

The mind, the primary controlling mechanism of the physical body, pushes the *pain confetti* all over our organs, bones, skin, and auric field. As it is the nature of the mind to seek relief from pain and suffering and to experience greater happiness, it is, therefore, helping to push out that suppressed energy in some form. Still, most often, the *confetti* gets stuck in our energetic, mental, and auric fields, manifesting in physical form as bodily disorders, mental and emotional illnesses, psychosomatic distress, chaotic behavior, and unhealthy interpersonal relationships.

This accumulated confetti of feelings, attachments, and emotions blocks our human evolution and growth as a spirit, prevents us from tapping into claiming our freedom, and keeps us stuck in many areas of our lives. It doesn't matter how many valuable practices we participate in, yoga courses, strengthening the nervous system with ice bathing, living in an ashram, spending hours in talk therapy, or rewilding the feminine; they will only give us partial liberation of pain. The stuck emotional *confetti* will continue to swirl in the emotional, mental, and auric fields until they are consciously discharged.

The Mind is Our Tool

For the practical application of our Grounding process, we utilize the mind to visualize the release of our pain. If the mind can create and hold thoughts of lack and unworthiness, take our emotional pain of attachment, convert it to feelings of fear, and shut down, then we can use that same mind to unwind the process and free ourselves from the emotional confetti of pain.

Yes, in this case, we *CAN* "solve a problem with the same mind that created it." We are using our mind as a means by which we release pain. We use our mind's eye to create images and visuals of tools that work on releasing the confetti of stuck pain and attachments in our physical and emotional bodies.

AMUSEMENT BREAK

I once submitted 10 puns to a joke competition. I really thought with that many, one was sure to be a winner. Sadly, no pun in ten did.

If your house is cold, just stand in the corner. It's always 90 degrees there.

I stayed up all night wondering where the sun went, and then it dawned on me.

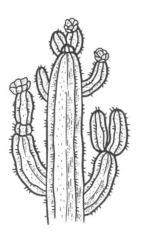

The Pain

"Everything you've ever wanted is sitting
on the other side of fear."

Fear

Fear is a powerful emotion. Fear often is the armor
that wraps around an immensely painful experience.
Fear is pain, personified. Fear is the facade that hides
the pain. Fear is so pandemic in our society that it
makes up the central ruling emotion of our world as
we know it. For many, fear is so omnipresent that their
life reality becomes one giant obstacle course intended
to conquer their fears. Instagram and YouTube are
filled with motivational gurus teaching you to break
through your fears. Using force to break up the pain

can leave the person unprepared to face the overwhelming gush of pain that comes exploding in.

The fear of facing the fear of reliving that excruciating, painful experience again causes many to stuff their pain away from awareness into the subconscious using disassociating, repetitive behavior, numbing, addiction, and so forth. In both cases, the *pain confetti* spills into the consciousness as overt anxiety attacks or phobias, antisocial or neurotic behaviors, resulting in a diagnosis of neurosis.

Curious to note that for over 15 years tranquilizer Diazepam has been the most prescribed drug in America. So many people are looking for ways to handle their pain. I wish for more people to discover the practice of Conscious Grounding to claim personal power over handling the physical, emotional, and mental manifestations of their stuck energy.

We often create a catch-22 cycle of repetition. By recoiling from facing our painful experiences, we attract similar experiences that hold the same vibration as the pain we are afraid to touch. By ignoring the pain confetti, we end up multiplying it. This causes the stuck pain, the pain confetti, to grow and escalate. What started with a few phobias or anxiety progressively spreads into more and more avenues of life, leading to further and further restrictions of activity and, in severe cases, to total immobilization.

Recoiling From Pain

This is understandable. If you burn your hand by mistakenly picking up a hot pan from the stove, your mind registers this, making your hand recoil in protection to remove you from the object of pain. *Pain confetti* is then created and added to the floating space of your energetic and mental *lava lamp*. When you come near another pan again, even one that is not hot, that energetic charge stored in that pain confetti will match the perceived reality, causing you to recoil from that pan. This happens whether you are consciously aware of it or not. The pain confetti holds such energetic attention, and as you know, "where attention goes, energy flows."

Now imagine how many stuck pain experiences are flowing in your energetic and mental space—anything from stubbing your toe to getting your heart broken. Our mind is designed for protection and uses those *confetti* memories to divert us from the experiences it perceives as harmful. That is unless we consciously clear that pain and claim our freedom from those stuck emotions.

In this exploration, we look at pain as the accumulation of stuck energy that shows up in your physical and emotional bodies as confetti. Some of that confetti can hold truly traumatic experiences, experiences so intense that you have refused to think, deal with, look at, or process for years and years. This is yet another reason why you are invited to step into the level of kindergarten and play when "working" with your pain.

An array of colorful confetti floating around the space is fun for a child. It helps remove the charge of processing it.

A Jitterbug?

Because this can be a loaded topic to read, let's take an amusement break. Before we continue, we *mustache* you a few questions. *"What is the best way to catch a fish? [Have someone throw it to you, of course.]"* And something fitting to our above discussion: *"What do you call an anxious fly? [A jitterbug.]" "What do kids play when they have nothing else to do? [Bored games.]"*

Even if you were raised in an emotionally supportive, loving household, you are still not immune to having energy stuck in your body. Society has begun to teach children and adults how to acknowledge pain through verbal validation, physical touch like hugging, and even the wonderful somatic practices of movement and dance. They help. They prepare your physical body to loosen the pain and stuck stress, but the emotional pain confetti remains floating in your mental and energetic space. We are not yet widely taught how to process the pain residue fully.

Completing the Loop

Grounding completes this loop by liberating any stuck pain confetti from an experience or negative emotion that created the block. By releasing pain from your body through Grounding, you create your own freedom in wholeness, in physical, emotional, and mental layers.

NOTES & OBSERVATIONS

Saṁskāra

Let's take the kindergarten concept of *pain confetti* presented in this guide a little further by looking into the teachings of Eastern Philosophies. Ancient schools of Yogic traditions have a concept referred to as *Saṁskāra*. Originating from Sanskrit, where *Saṁ* means complete or interconnected, and *Kāra* denotes action, cause, or doing. This notion of *Saṁskāra* holds significant importance across various major schools of Hindu philosophy, Buddhism, and Jainism. According to these ancient teachings, we inherit a karmic legacy of mental and emotional patterns, *Saṁskāras*, which we continuously cycle through during our lifetime.

Yogic traditions offer differing perspectives on how *Samskāra* operates at the subconscious level.

Ancient Perspectives on Samskāra

In Buddhism, *Samskāra* is viewed as *causal continua*, aligning with its fundamental premise of *no self, no soul*. It is seen as a continuum of causes and effects rather than being tied to any enduring self or entity.

On the other hand, within Vedic traditions of Hinduism, *Samskāra* is understood as *relational properties* residing within an individual's Self or Soul. These are impressions, marks, impulses, or tendencies that influence one's psychological makeup and potential energy.

In Hindu philosophies such as Yoga, Vedanta, and Nyaya, *Samskāra* is an affective and motivational force that shapes one's value structure. These philosophies endorse inner drives that consciously or subconsciously propel future actions, thoughts, judgments, and premises.

Despite these variations in interpretation, *Samskāra* remains a fundamental concept in understanding the psychological and spiritual dimensions of human existence across these philosophical traditions.

Development of Samskāra

Every experience we encounter involves a multitude of factors, including sensory perceptions such as sight, sound, taste, smell, touch, and the workings of the mind itself (*here mind becomes a sixth sense*). These experiences elicit one of three possible outcomes: they can be positive, negative, or neutral in nature.

When an experience is particularly pleasurable or painful, it leaves an imprint on the mind. This impression, known as *Saṁskāra*, becomes embedded within the *Citta*, or subconscious mind. Over time— whether it be days, months, or even years—these dormant impressions can be triggered by memory, activating the *Saṁskāra* and prompting a desire to seek out or avoid a similar experience. Repetition of such experiences further reinforces the *Saṁskāra*.

This process sheds light on why thoughts, desires, and emotions often arise in our minds seemingly without our conscious control—they are manifestations of the latent subconscious content that resides within us, continually influencing our perceptions and responses to the world around us.

Habitual Reinforcement

As *Saṁskāras* continue to be repeated and reinforced, a habitual pattern of behavior referred to as *Vāsana* forms. Some of these habitual patterns, *Vāsanas,* are actively cultivated and necessary for our societal functioning.

For instance, consider the complex skill of driving, which involves learning road rules, understanding traffic signs and signals, mastering vehicle control, and being aware of other vehicles and pedestrians. This process demands focused learning, concentration, and repeated practice. Once these skills are internalized and transformed into a *Vāsana*, driving becomes almost instinctual—allowing us to navigate traffic while engaging in other activities like conversations, listening to music, or contemplating various matters.

While positive *Saṁskāras* and *Vāsanas* are crucial for our effective functioning as individuals, there are also negative *Saṁskāras* that lead to suffering and hinder our efficiency. These negative *Saṁskāras* often serve as defense and avoidance mechanisms to protect our egos. We must address and work with these negative patterns in our spiritual practices, referred to as *Sādhana* in the Yogic traditions, to promote personal growth and alleviate suffering.

Activation of Saṁskāras

Recall and activation of *Saṁskāras* can occur through four primary methods:

1. **Spontaneous Recall:** Sometimes, *Saṁskāras* are spontaneously triggered without any deliberate effort. These activations can happen seemingly out of nowhere, often in response to external stimuli or internal associations.

2. **Voluntary Recall:** In this method, individuals intentionally summon specific memories or experiences from their subconscious mind. This conscious effort to recall *Saṁskāras* can be useful in various contexts, such as problem-solving or decision-making.

3. **Involuntary Recall:** Unlike voluntary recall, involuntary recall involves the sudden and unexpected emergence of *Saṁskāras* into conscious awareness. These activations may occur due to triggers in the external environment or internal mental states, such as emotions or sensations.

4. **Dream Recall:** During sleep, the mind often accesses and processes *Saṁskāras* through dreams. Upon waking, individuals may recall these dream experiences, which can provide insights into their subconscious thoughts, emotions, and desires.

These four recall methods play a significant role in activating and manifesting *Saṁskāras*, influencing our thoughts, behaviors, and perceptions in various ways.

Saṁskāras Prompts in Sanskrit

1. *Smṛti hetu* – the perception of any sensory input related to an object or occasion can trigger recollection through the five senses

2. *Sadṛśata* – when observing objects that bear a resemblance to each other can prompt recollection

3. *Viparītata* – opposite connotation – e.g., A lavish meal reminds one of hunger

4. *Kārya-kārana-sambandha* – relation between cause and effect, e.g., A fallen tree reminds one of a storm

Saṁskāras Formation

According to the Vedas (*ancient Hindu scriptures, believed to have been directly revealed to seers, and preserved by oral tradition*)   there are six stages for formation of *Saṁskāras*

1. *Kriya* - the act

2. *Anubhava* - the experience of feelings of positivity, negativity, or neutrality

3. *Saṁskāra* - the impression formed in the mind that gradually embeds itself into the subconscious mind

4. *Vāsana* - the repetition of the initial action and experiencing its outcomes repeatedly, either a positive inclination *Rāga* or a negative aversion *Dveṣa* is strengthened as a habitual tendency

5. *Iccha* - the desire nature that constitutes a fundamental aspect of our character

6. *Tṛṣṇa* —when desire nature is consistently indulged in, it transforms into entrenched cravings and drives that significantly influence our actions. This objectified desire often manifests as a sense of obsessing and clinging to the desired object. The stronger the attachment, the greater the degree of suffering, *Duḥkha,* we experience.

Relationship to Karma

The accumulation of *Saṁskāras*, whether positive or negative, forms our mental disposition or *Svabhāva*. Neutral acts and experiences typically leave vague mental impressions of little consequence unless reinforced by repeated practice.

A predominance of positive *Saṁskāras* cultivates a positive mental disposition, while an excess of negative *Saṁskāras* may lead to a negative, fearful, or tormented disposition.

According to the Yogic Philosophy, at the moment of death, our dominant disposition, or *Svabhāva*, determines our next rebirth and its circumstances. Thus, when the physical body is shed, the consciousness, laden with *Saṁskāras*, takes on another body in alignment with the nature of those *Saṁskāras*.

In essence, the bodies we are born with, the circumstances surrounding our birth, and significant life events are all products of our previous thought-streams. This underscores the principle: *As you think, so you become **yad bhāvam tad bhavati!*** Therefore, it is encouraged to introspect and modify our actions to cultivate a positive state of mind characterized by contentment, peace, compassion, and generosity while avoiding emotions like anger, resentment, aggression, violence, fear, and anxiety.

Dealing with Negative Saṁskāras

Dealing with negative *Saṁskāras* involves practices such as objective introspection, self-auditing *Svadhyāya,* and meditation like the Grounding practice discussed in this guide.

During Grounding practice, as we allow Earth's gravitational pull to free our physical, mental, and emotional bodies of the *Saṁskāras* or stuck emotional pain, we may also observe various astonishing and shocking images arising in our minds. However, we maintain neutrality and continue to Ground and release the pain, allowing these thoughts to pass without getting entangled in them. We refrain from analyzing or engaging with them, simply acknowledging their presence and letting them go as we return to our point of focus. Despite their potential intensity, we continue to observe them with detachment and release them.

This process requires consistent practice and patience to cultivate. Additionally, supportive friends who can kindly point out faults and negativity can greatly aid personal development.

Saṁskāras and Pain Confetti

The introduction of *Saṁskāras* into this guide illustrates how ancient this concept is and is a homage to my *Right of Passage* years with the Vedic Philosophy. I have spent over two cumulative years living in Indian ashrams studying the Vedas, including Yoga, Ayurveda, and Sanskrit. Although my learning of the Yogic teachings spans three decades, I will need a lifetime, or more, to even begin grasping the vastness of its wisdom.

For this reason, I like to approach spirituality and ancient wisdom through the lens of childlike wonder, the level of kindergarten. This is why the core of this guide is presented in more playful ways, using terms like *pain confetti.*

AMUSEMENT BREAK

The owner of the tuxedo store kept hovering over me when I was browsing, so I asked him to leave me alone. He said, "Fine, suit yourself."

I found a book called How to Solve 50% of Your Problems. So I bought 2.

Your Freedom and Your Answers

The self-help, spiritual "industry" is a multi-billion machine for obvious reasons: more and more people crave a more purposeful life, fulfillment, and personal freedom. Many people are habituated to seek these answers on the external, outside of themselves. Be it coming from Judeo-Christian societies, or Hindu, Islam, agnostic intellectual circles, etc, the centuries-engraved pathways to finding G O D (answers) were through the *learnits*, priests, pundits, or people of knowledge. The gurus are there waiting to "liberate you."

Do you know how many "spiritual" teachers will take your power from you and how fast they will do so? A person on an authentic quest for answers, desiring to reconnect with their heart, is ripe fruit for the plucking by those claiming to know the way.

Everyone Has an Agenda

Swamis, yogis, PhDs, goddesses, priestesses, and shamans, even the ones claiming they are not your guru, often say so with an agenda of hooking you into their program, which only gets better with your repeated attendance.

As was shared earlier, the ones who take your power are not always gurus or self-help influencers. Marketers, alternative theorists, songwriters, and even movies have a way to hook into your energy and take away your freedom. They push your buttons and trigger your pain.

They know just the right *confetti* to highlight to get you hooked. Are you going through a breakup, unemployed, or suffering from low self-esteem? Do you fear public speaking, disagree with this politician, can't find love, or experience emotional blockages in your heart? "I'll fix you, they say! I have your answers." So you go to them, work their program, and drink their tea. Your problems seem to fade away, and a euphoria kicks in.

Becoming Programmable

You speak with words from their lexicon and quote their names when sharing stories. Your identity becomes tied to being a part of their program, school, community, university, exclusive club, etc. You remain hooked because the *pain confetti* in your physical, mental, and emotional layers has not been released. They still have a hold over you.

You think you have received the answer to your question from this external source, but it is a crutch propping you up, making you think you are standing on your own. Even if you switch from one program, one modality to something seemingly completely different, you continue to give away your freedom until those pain confetti control your energetic vibrations. Yes, the pain in your emotional body is that powerful. Your own answers remain muffled by the pain.

How to be Discerning

How do you know if what's being presented is a genuine sharing of knowledge or tools or if it carries an alternative motive of claiming your power? This guide doesn't have that answer for you.

This guide shows you what vibrational frequencies create openness to finding your truth. It provides practices and tools you can use to liberate yourself from pain confetti and free yourself from blockages preventing you from seeing your truth. This guide shows you the door; the rest is up to you. The answers are there for you to discover.

You Have The Answer

All of this is not to say that having a teacher is wrong. All of this is to say that YOU have the answer. It's in you! You have it. The guru, the pastor, and the coach do not have it for you. A true teacher will show you the way. They can give you the tools and show you *their* way of understanding, but your answer is in you. The less *pain confetti* you have, the less others can control, trigger, or manipulate you. If there are no buttons, there is nothing to push.

Cherish and protect that authentic quest for answers that ignites your heart and propels you forward in your quest. Don't give anyone your power. Use your discernment to check with your inner knowing if something is true for YOU.

The process of Grounding and connecting to Earth shared in this guide is a tool to find your liberation and answers. It is the tool through which you polish your discernment by clearing the pain energy and thought patterns of others in your space. Every time you release pain confetti from your physical, mental, and energetic space, you kick out people's thoughts, programs, and opinions that have meddled with your true, authentic knowing. You get your power and freedom back, and when you do, don't give it to anyone, ever.

Introduction to Grounding

What is Grounding?

In simple terms, Grounding is creating an energetic connection from your body to the center of the planet. This is done to feel safe in your body, feel connected to the planet we live on, and have a means of moving energy out of space.

Grounding is a visceral full-body experience that delivers holistic integration—physically, mentally, and spiritually—while harmonizing with the Earth's energies. It involves a deep level of unity encompassing all facets of oneself. When your physical body becomes energetically linked to the

Earth's force, every interaction within the third dimension undergoes a transformation, offering a wholly new perspective on life.

The visualization process of Conscious Grounding and releasing pain is the single most transformative method in your toolbox.

Upon repeated use, one begins to recognize the sensation of liberation. At times, the feeling is as strong as releasing the steam from a pressure cooker. Other times, it is the smooth flow of a waterfall. With that comes a sense of inner strength, centeredness, and balance. As you release stuck pain confetti, a fresh sense of freedom, solace, and harmony becomes available. Grounding is available to anyone, anywhere, and anytime. As you remove the energetic charge of stuck pain, you can shift the reality around you. You can switch timelines.

An alternative definition of Grounding is establishing an energetic link that anchors and safeguards your individual life force energy to the life force energy of the Earth.

Shifting Reality Timeline

This hypothetical shift of timeline reality is a paraphrased example from a personal experience tested repeatedly using and not using Grounding. While you can't control how others act or react around you, you can gain control of what is happening in your reality, and what and how you engage with it.

❜❜ Say your mother stops by your house unannounced. You know from your previous experiences that she will try to push your buttons, and you will get triggered, react, and engage in an argument. In this hypothetical example, your mother's pain confetti has an energetic match to your pain confetti, creating an ideal scenario of a charged fight. Without conscious Grounding, you may become triggered and irritated the moment you realize your mother is at the door. You will try to compose yourself and maintain decorum, saying to yourself that your spiritually enlightened, learned self can behave like a mature adult and visit with your mother. Then, you catch the way your mother looked at your messy bed, which you perceive as judgment, and your triggers set off. Your pain confetti of previous experiences of unworthiness matches your mother's pain confetti of being abandoned and set off a firework. The

bottled-up energy seems discharged as you throw your pain confetti onto each other. You walk away feeling guilty and ashamed but also euphoric. Your mind is creating new pain confetti connected to this experience, amplifying a belief that your mother is a narcissistic vampire.

But can this scenario play out differently? Say you are sitting on a couch watching a movie and see your mother at the door. You notice a trigger of irritation about your mother stopping by unannounced. You then pause and recognize that you are getting triggered. You laugh at yourself in amusement at being triggered by something as trivial as a casual pop-in. A laugh out loud helps you take control of your reality.

As your mother comes up the stairs, you take your time to visualize Grounding to first yourself, and then to your mother. As you open your door, you feel yourself being in amused neutrality, with pain confetti swooshing away from your energetic and mental space. Your mother walks in, and you notice her frown at your unmade bed, but she instantly smiles and says she is glad you are finally giving yourself a day off to relax. She leaves the soup she brought for you on a table and realizes that she needs to run out quickly as her favorite grocery store is about to close. How miraculous is this? You free yourself from stuck emotional pain, discharge the energy of your mother becoming reactive to you, and continue enjoying your movie with a hot soup.

This is what this simple process of visualizing the release of pain is all about. Conscious and frequent Grounding puts you in control of how you feel and clear where your energies end, and others begin. You free yourself from buttons that can be pushed to trigger you or solicit a reaction. You just shrug your shoulders in amusement as you are simply, truly, and wholly unbothered.

Helpful Suggestions

Here are a few suggestions to help you ground more easily, especially during your first introductions into the practice, to make your grounding experience enjoyable.

Claim your space both literally and figuratively.

Find a cozy private space where you will feel comfortable and safe.

While getting familiar with Grounding, be **seated in a chair with your legs uncrossed** (*this part is important, as it keeps the energy flow pulsing from the*

Earth through your body), your back straight.

Sitting in a lotus position is not ideal for this practice, as it cuts the meridian pathways and does not permit the energy to flow freely from the Earth.

T ake a full, delicious breath to bring all aspects of yourself into harmony. Nourish your body with air all the way into the pelvic bone.

L ook around the room and notice something close or far away from you. This brings you into the present moment and soothes your nervous system by helping you find safety.

S et a dedicated time. 15-20 minutes is a good start. For the next 15-20 minutes, you don't have to worry about anything else but what is happening now. Put the phone on silent. This time is now fully and completely yours.

N otice and observe your body. Observe any tension, pain, or discomfort without trying to fix or judge anything.

R epeated Grounding practice helps you develop a brand new relationship with your body and spirit based on trust and personal self-worth. You are consciously taking the time for yourself to heal and take back control over your freedom.

Choose an Anchor

Choose an object, a scent, or an art form you bring as part of your Grounding practice. This can be anything, but it's best if it is the same thing you can use every time. For me, it is one of my skincare products I apply before my Grounding practice. Every time I smell that product now, my energy immediately shifts into a state of Grounding and harmony. You can choose a crystal to hold or a special essential oil blend. Train your mind to connect that scent/object with your Grounding practice. It will then act as a catalyst in reminding you to ground and how good it feels in your body when you ground and meditate.

Grounding is Simple

This Grounding practice involves visualization and is best accessed through childlike wonder and creativity. Remember kindergarten we talked about earlier in this guide?

Floating in Bright Stars

When I was seven years old, I remember my father lifting his head from the guide he was reading and asking me, seemingly out of nowhere, if I could imagine being surrounded by flames. This sounded exciting to me, so I did, telling my dad how I see orange and red flames dancing around my body. I think he was reading the volumes of Agni Yoga, where they discussed transcendental abilities of mind over matter and how children have an innate ability to "make up states" and transcend time and space.

My astounded father then asked if I could imagine a bright light of millions of stars moving through my arms, legs, and torso and then flowing through my entire body, transforming me into a bright star myself. His descriptions of being a star were so fun that I immediately propped up and began to visualize.

That experience was over 30 years ago, and I still remember it as if it just happened. I could feel the flow of stars through my arms. My feet and palms began to tingle. Then, as I laughed and continued to imagine it, my entire body tingled with light. That was so fun. It was my first introduction to running energies through my body, and I often return to that child-like wonder and joy I experienced in that moment.

pre scriptum

Finding sitting meditation challenging? Join me on my podcast where I share "grounding in motion" www.mahalo.care/podcast/

Grounding, the Practice

Don't Be So Serious

B e seated in a chair, with your feet flat on the ground, back straight, and hands comfortably on your lap.

N otice your body. Permit yourself to relax. See if you can feel the flow of star energy pulsing and tingling in your feet, arms, legs, torso, neck, and so on. Resist judgment if you do not feel this yet. The meridians are the pathways through which *prana/ mana/chi/*life force energy flows through your body. By bringing your attention to it, you connect to that force.

I n your mind's eye, create (visualize) a mental picture of whatever you'd like to use for your Grounding cord. This can be a picture of anything from a giant redwood tree, a waterfall, a ship's anchor chain, a stack of cupcakes, or a pirate's treasure chest of gold. The more amusement this brings you, the easier it will be to release pain as we use the cord in the process, so have fun.

A s you visualize, attach the top of your Grounding cord to the first energy center (chakra) at the base of your spine (located near the coccygeal plexus).

A llow gravity to take your Grounding cord all the way to the center of the Earth. Imagine the stack of cupcakes (*use your visualized image of the Grounding cord here*) multiplying as they fly into the boiling magma at the planet's core. Feel the Grounding cord connecting your energies to that of the Earth.

I magine (visualize) a light switch that you can flip to "on," setting your Grounding cord to "release" and allow gravity to drain the pain confetti out of your body. It flows out of the body like water down a drain with no effort.

S pend as much time as you are comfortable consciously Grounding in this position. The longer you sit connected to the core of the Earth, the more *prana*/energy will flow through your body, and the more nourished and pain-free you will become.

You might feel a sudden discomfort, agitation, and a strong desire to get up from the chair and cut off the Grounding. You are invited to continue to sit through these feelings, as they indicate that an energetic blockage of pain confetti is working its way out of your system. This will pass as suddenly as it appeared.

The longer you are able to sit in your conscious Grounding practice, the more pain blockages you are able to move out of your body.

Before completing the practice, give a mental tug on your Grounding cord and thank it for helping you claim your freedom. Once set, this Grounding cord will continue to release energy for 24-48 hours.

*If you would like to follow guided meditation, you are welcome to listen to my audio recording. Scan a **QR code** below, or follow these links:*

www.merinaeldan.com/groundingaudio/

www.mahalo.care/podcast/

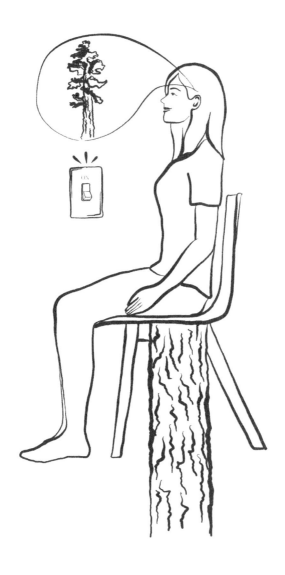

Keeping It Simple

By being continuously grounded, it is possible to remain in a state of freedom and neutrality. Thoughts come and go, and feelings arise. You bump into things like a photo of you and your ex-partner or an aggravated neighbor in an elevator. But as you remain connected to the energies of the Earth, gravity clears any pain confetti from your Being.

You notice that you remain unfazed by an experience that used to trigger you. You become a neutral observer of the events happening around you. This time, however, you remain an observer, not through disassociation or checking out, but by being wholly and completely embodied in the present moment. You can then become amused by your neighbor constantly being aggravated about the slow elevator or the rainy weather.

As the Grounding practice becomes an intrinsic part of your life, you get closer and closer to the authentic Self and begin to see that so much of what you thought was real was actually a duplicitous layer of pain all along.

A Tool for All

The fun in this process is that it works for the enlightened, the cynic, the spiritualist, the academic, the atheist, the religionist, and the normalist. No matter how new or advanced you are on your spiritual or well-being path, Grounding will continuously support and surprise you. It is a tool best approached with a freshness of a child-like wonder every time. *What will the Grounding have in store for me today?* An ice cream, a free first-class upgrade on a plane, calm traffic to work, or a liberation of a century-old family trauma?

"Truth is ever to be found in simplicity, and not in the multiplicity and confusion of things. " — Sir Isaac Newton.

This is most true with this Grounding technique. The simplicity of its process might cause some people to disregard its potential. The marketing machine has conditioned us to think that something that costs more, takes longer, or requires more work will naturally produce better quality, have more value, and deliver a superior result. Years and years of talk therapy, intense retreats, or drinking hallucinogenic plants releasing fluids from all orifices.

Showing the Way

All that hard work is how you feel you "deserve" to be liberated from your pain. You are working for it. Then comes this guide with a notion of kindergarten play and a Grounding tool that just drains away your pain. Surely, it can't be that simple. Maybe it is, maybe it isn't. The job of this guide is to show you the way, and to invite you to come play with it yourself.

Every time you consciously engage in the practice of Grounding, every time you connect your physical body with the Earth, you are opening yourself up to a possibility of wonder. You put yourself in the position to control your own energy.

Looking After Your Grounding Cord

Your Grounding cord will continue to release and do its work for 24 - 48 hours after you have consciously stepped away from practice. With time, changing the Grounding cord will be as easy as changing your socks.

When sitting down in practice, like described above, bring yourself into a relaxed state, focus on your first energy center (chakra), and see the Grounding cord you plugged in the last time you grounded.

Do you "see" it? Do you get *a knowing* of it? Is it tired and ready to be unplugged? Detach it and, with the help of Earth's gravity, send it down into the boiling center of magma.

Visualize a new Grounding cord. How about something you have not used before, a giant quartz crystal, a stack of raspberries, or maybe a string of pearls the size of a small dog? Find amusement and joy in your Grounding cord's shape, color, or material. Attach it to the first energy center (chakra), and flip it "on" release for gravity to continue to do its work.

Size of your Grounding Cord

You can play with the size of the Grounding cord as much as you like. Generally, the wider you can make your Grounding cord, the more energy it can hold, and the more solid you will feel. When first working on widening your Grounding cord, imagine a redwood. Some ancient redwood trees are as wide as 10-40 feet in diameter. Use that size as your Grounding cord, and notice how solid you feel in your body.

Strengthening Your Grounding Cord

In addition to widening your Grounding cord, sometimes it is good to refresh or strengthen it. The easiest way to do this is to raise its frequency by visualizing pouring a bucket of pure rose essential oil down the cord. Rose has the highest vibrational frequency in the plant world. When you match your Grounding cord to the vibration of a rose, you are clearing it from other people's energies and increasing the flow of gravity, clearing your pain and stuck energy.

Benefits of Grounding

You can begin applying Grounding into practice now. Following the Grounding practice flow from the earlier chapter, allow your body to remain connected to the Earth. Let gravity take away the pain while keeping you solid and centered. We will check in and remind you to say hello to your current Grounding cord or, if it has been more than 24-48 hours, to create a new one as we journey forward.

Radio-frequency

There was a time in the early broadcasting days when we listened to AM radio, which was available only as a MONO sound. The transmitted sound was short and unreliable, filled with pop, crackle, and static. Had you tried to listen to the AM radio, you would have had to constantly adjust the receiver to maintain the chosen frequency. If you were driving at night, in most cases, you could only listen to the "clear channel" stations because they were the only ones broadcasting at a higher frequency and could travel long distances and maintain their strength.

In the 1970s, radio broadcasting was upgraded to stereo frequency. Sound was deeper, and the signals were much more far-reaching. This technology removed the earlier years' screeching static of the mono AM radio.

In the 1990s, technology saw an even bigger boost with streaming services. In the 2000s, people could suddenly download and listen to music on their phones. Music freed itself from the confinements of radio. It was now accessible on computers, tablets, and appliances such as streaming and podcasting. The delivered sound is now full, nuanced, and as real as hearing it firsthand.

Energy as a Radio-frequency

This example of transmitted sound frequency perfectly applies to the effects and benefits of Grounding. When we only had AM transmissions in MONO frequency, it was hard to imagine that the sound could be anything else because we didn't know anything else.

Similarly, when a person does not use the tools of Grounding to clear their *pain confetti*, they can't imagine they can feel any different. Grounding clears the static, crackling, and pop of AM frequencies, as well as the emotional triggers, anxiety, and inability to distinguish between where an individual's voice ends and the pain begins.

When we begin to ground, free ourselves from pain, and create space from stuck energy, we begin to hear sounds in stereo and FM quality. Our authentic voice begins to emerge. The more we ground and clear pain, the clearer our individual voice becomes, and the more freedom is gained. Soon, we are no longer relying on external support for answers. The need for "radio to transmit the sound" is no longer required. We are able to be in our own energy, and our own authenticity, broadcasting/podcasting authenticity to ourselves and the world.

Success in Life

The more you connect your body to the Earth, the safer your body will feel, and the stronger the relationship between your body and spirit will be. When I think of a Grounded person, I imagine someone radiating a strength that affords them self-mastery, exhibiting presence in a practical and focused way. People who Ground regularly experience more ease in life, with flow, clear communication, smooth relationships, and an increased ability to manifest their goals. They tend to handle their responsibilities with efficiency and grace, often enjoying repeated success. I have been able to witness this many times, professionally and personally.

Increased Emotional Intelligence

As you remain connected to the energies of the Earth through the Grounding cord, which is similar to having your doctor or therapist on speed dial with you, you are directly linked to the ultimate source of healing—Earth. You will sometimes notice when your emotions go out of alignment within seconds. You get an almost precognitive view of a situation where you might be triggered simply because the Grounding cord is doing its job of freeing you from the emotional pain triggers as soon as they get stirred up in your subconscious.

Protection

Grounding is an excellent way to protect yourself from external circumstances in your immediate surroundings. If you are in a meeting at work, doing dishes in your kitchen at home, or driving in a car and suddenly hear the loud sound of emergency sirens, an alarm sounds in your body. Although beneficial at alerting us of possible danger, they also set off our nervous system into a varied level of panicked response. The sound is designed to alarm and alert us.

As you check your surroundings, you realize on a conscious level that no danger is happening or is about to happen to you. However, your subconscious and nervous system, and with them the adrenaline/pain confetti, are thrown into panic. Your hands might tremble, your body may begin to perspire, your pupils dilate, and you might experience shortness of breath. Images of car crashes, burning buildings, and other traumatic events seen in real life or on TV flash before your eyes. In short, you have experienced a trigger.

Hearing the sound of an emergency siren is an excellent time to Ground, and to Ground right away. Connect your physical and energetic bodies to those of the Earth, consciously connect to the Grounding cord, and allow it to release all those neurotic physical responses, all those fear and pain images, all those triggers, the pain confetti. Grounding protects you from being affected by external circumstances in your immediate surroundings. You don't have to align to the panic of emergency sirens if they do not impact you directly.

Your Goal-Actualizing Abilities Soar

When you are grounded, you connect to the supreme expert being level of manifestors in physical form—Earth. Mother Earth is a being, and Her manifestation abilities are beyond expert level. Out of all other planets in our system, She was able to manifest having humans as actualized potential energy in a physical form.

When we connect to Her energies through the Grounding cord, we learn and are supported by the supreme master of all. She helps us release pain and create more space and freedom in our bodies, and we fill that newly created space with our goals and desires.

Increased Artistic Abilities

There is an unspoken knowing among people of creative talent that their artistic inspiration is often an "elusive mistress," coming and going on her own accord. Some artists say they are learning to remove "themselves" from the creative process to allow the creative muse to take over. In simpler terms, the removal of "themselves" they are referring to is the clearing of the pain confetti, the triggers, the stuck energy that does not allow for the Divine creative juices to flow through them. With Grounding, they can remain in a more constant state of space and freedom, allowing their artistic abilities to take more forms and expressions.

Grounding in Daily Life

The results of Grounding are deceptively quick and subtle, but the effects are very powerful. Grounding can also be done anywhere, anytime, and with anything: sitting, lying down, walking, climbing, standing, running, or even while flying in an airplane. You can also ground a car, computer, or any electronic device (*especially handy during Mercury retrograde for those especially charged*), a person, a situation, a movie, and, of course, any and all memories from your past.

A Back Pain for the Holidays

// Early in December last year, Natalie and her family of three plus a cat were notified that their apartment had sold and a new owner was to take occupancy at the beginning of the month. Her very sensitive three-year-old son did not adjust easily to changes. With the holidays just a few weeks away, the need to find a place that allowed pets, pack their entire house, and then move was a very overwhelming experience.

Natalie and her husband were realistic about their prospects. They lived in their rent-controlled apartment for over a decade, and with the neighborhood becoming gentrified in recent years, their rental options, should they be lucky enough to find one, would require almost double the amount of their current rent. Her stress was compounded by the overwhelming memories of her childhood when her parents lived in a studio apartment with a shared bathroom with a neighbor.

The repetitive thought of her sensitive son having to deal with the same situations as in her childhood kept Natalie up at night for a week. With all this worrying, her chronic back problem flared until, finally, she wasn't able to move. The stress of her mind locked up her body. But matters did not get easier here. The first available chiropractic appointment was the first week of the new year. Some closed early for the holidays, while the others were fully booked with current patients. It felt like the world was closing in on her, and Natalie was riddled with anxiety and pain.

You are likely to realize right now that since this story has made it onto the pages of the guide, Natalie has discovered the Grounding practice. You are right; she did. Her first experience was unremarkable, but she tried it again at her husband's insistence.

They sat together, although Natalie was on the bed, with her legs stretched out and the back propped up with pillows. They entered a calm state through breath and became aware of the present moment. They observed the room, noticing the small details of flowers embroidered on a quilt and the steam coming from the hot cup of tea. Natalie created an image of a Grounding cord in the shape of pinecones, as she felt the prickliness of the pinecones was a good representation of her agitation and anxiety, which made her smirk.

She then decided to dress those pinecones with old boots, fishing poles, and other random attic finds. Somehow, this visualization of decorating her Grounding cord with absurd items made her smile. It was the first time she felt a sense of humor in days. She followed her husband's instructions again, hooked up this grinch-like holiday Grounding cord under the bottom of her spine, and sent it swirling down to the center of the Earth. When he told her to make it wider, she laughed out loud, visualizing these stacked pinecones growing as big as the redwood trees.

She flipped the switch and asked Earth to take away her pain. She allowed gravity to do its work, taking away all the build-up of the emotional and pain confetti that had been swirling in her space. Natalie fell asleep as she released energy. She was awakened by her crying son in another room and got out of bed to check on him.

Only after she snuggled up with him did she realize in surprise that she had gotten out of bed after being immobile for a whole day. Her back pain was gone. Consciously participating in Grounding to release the build-up of stress from current events and the pain confetti of her childhood traumatic experiences done with amusement and non-attachment shifted her energy.

This was a pivotal moment for Natalie to reclaim her power and step into freedom by realizing "what above, so below." Experiencing the energy shifts, the emotional liberation she felt in her mind, and the disappearance of physical pain gave her a renewed sense of direction, opening the doors to what seemed impossible before.

Natalie and her husband moved out of the city to be closer to his parents. They found a house bigger than their apartment, with lower rent, and in a more family-friendly neighborhood. Their lives began to shift in a much more positive direction, with Grounding practice at their core, helping them remain neutral and open to life's possibilities.

Things You Can Do with Your Grounding Cord

Grounding is a tool that can be applied anytime, anywhere, with anything. Grounding allows you to shift energy so what was unseen suddenly becomes seen. What was impossible becomes possible-within reason, of course.

But say you can't find your car keys, and you frantically look around your purse, office, or bathroom. The energy is frazzled; the chaos confetti is everywhere. The noise of that energy static prevents you from knowing the right direction to turn.

You are spinning the wheels and the chaos sets in. Instead, pause, take a breath, and notice the chaos. Take control in settling the energy. Visualize your keys and create a Grounding cord under them. Ground the energy around you and yourself. Now open your eyes and look again. Voila, first try; the keys are by the fridge where you left them when unloading the groceries last night.

Grounding While Driving

It is usually not recommended to meditate while driving. But it is different with Grounding practices.

You can and are encouraged to ground your car before or while driving. Simply create a mental picture of a Grounding cord you want to use for your car (as simple as a redwood tree, a good faithful waterfall, or maybe a wrench or a stack of car tires). Bring the top of this Grounding cord under your car and hook it in. Drop it down to the center of the Earth and see gravity connect it with the core of the planet. Widen the visual of the cord to be as wide as the car, and flip it "on" to release.

When you release stuck energy around your car, you will notice that, somehow, your navigation system directs you around traffic. You arrive at your destination a few minutes early, and even your fuel seems to last longer.

Grounding Your Home

The energies of those around us impact us. We are even more impacted by the energies of our environment. Grounding your home is an especially great practice during family visits, holidays, or when you or a family member is sick.

Take a moment of mindfulness. Close your eyes, and nourish yourself by enjoying a delicious breath. With your eyes closed, visualize the four walls of your house. Trace one wall, and visualize it extending beyond foundation into Earth and further down to the center of the planet. Continue with the second, third, and fourth walls of the house, dropping each wall from the bottom into the core of the Earth. Take it a step further by visualizing your "on" switch, flipping it to release all negative and stagnant energy in the space. Similar to how our houses are grounded to allow for lightning bolts to pass through to the Earth, you are doing the same process with all unwanted energies.

When your home is grounded, you will notice a much calmer atmosphere, less agitated animals, more playful kids, and even plants seem more lively and green. The energy of your home will be more alive.

Grounding While Watching TV

This is an excellent way to have you LOVE the Grounding process. Especially if the movie you are watching is something that brings you pleasure. This is also an opportunity to practice Grounding while lying down or lounging. You don't have to always Ground while sitting down; just make sure your legs are not crossed so you don't block the flow of energy. The rest is the same. Cozy-up on the couch or bed.

87

Breathe in, create a mental image of a Grounding cord (what about trying popcorn), connect it to your first energy center, and let gravity take your popcorn Grounding cord to the core of the Earth. Flip it "on" release, and enjoy clearing out stuck energy and pain while you watch your show.

An alternative use of Grounding while watching TV is protecting yourself from the manipulative information transmitted to you from the show, program, or movie. By connecting yourself to Earth's energy field and allowing gravity to take away information coming your way, you remain neutral and not programmable. You are now grounded and free to enjoy rather than absorb the program or show.

Grounding Your Money

Wallace Stevens once eloquently expressed that "Money is a form of poetry." Indeed, money, like everything else, carries its own energetic essence. The next time you find yourself amidst nature, engaged in meditation, consider bringing along your wallet, checkbook, or credit/debit card, placing them before you. Close your eyes, and visualize grounding these financial tools to the core of the earth. Take a moment to discern whose energies are on your bank account. Is this vibrational frequency conducive to your aspirations, or does it emanate from a place of lack imposed by others?

When receiving money from others, are you attuned to its energetic imprint? I recall a birthday where I was gifted a hundred-dollar bill, yet its energy was far from neutral. Laden with "stop" signals and invalidating vibes, it disrupted the self-checkout machine at the supermarket. Receiving money becomes far simpler when it arrives energetically neutral, devoid of undue burden or expectations.

How do you envision receiving money? From what vibrational frequency? Perhaps ease and fluidity? Engaging in the Grounding of your financial space constitutes an integral facet of ongoing energy work, fostering self-support and alignment.

Grounding Your Relationships

During your next Grounding meditation, visualize a space, say a bubble, symbolizing your relationship space to a spouse, friend, family member, coworker, or desired relationship you wish to be in. Visualize a Grounding cord (be creative and playful here) and attach it to the bottom of the visualized relationship bubble. Flip the switch "on" to release stuck energy in your relationship space.

For those already in a relationship, grounding this symbolic bubble can foster enhanced communication and connection with your partner. If you find yourself unattached, this practice serves as a powerful tool to cultivate space for a new relationship to blossom. It's likely that you wouldn't want your parents' expectations or energies infiltrating your romantic relationship space; grounding them out is a straightforward process. Grounding your relationship space aids in shedding old narratives from past or current relationships, allowing you to approach relationship patterns with a newfound sense of neutrality. This neutrality empowers you to consciously shape the dynamics of your relationships according to your desires.

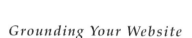

Grounding Your Website

When people visit your website, they often project energies of judgments, opinions, expectations, demands, curiosities, and fears onto it. Over time, these diverse energies accumulate, potentially obscuring the original energetic essence of your website from new visitors' perspectives. Engaging in simple Grounding of these external energies can effectively cleanse your virtual space, allowing the authentic message to shine through and attract new clients.

Grounding each page of your website serves as a practical method to reset its vibration to a positive frequency. This practice also sheds light on why business owners may periodically seek to revamp their entire website. As someone who once owned a branding and design agency, I often pondered why managers and business owners sought to alter visually appealing websites seemingly without cause. However, it becomes clear that their motivation often lies in resetting the energetic atmosphere, albeit without necessarily understanding alternative methods beyond reconstructing the website from scratch. Therefore, regularly tending to the energetic dynamics of your website and business facets is crucial for maintaining a positive virtual presence and attracting clients.

Grounding Your Pets

I have the loveliest dog named Luna. When she was one year old she was diagnosed with an idiopathic epilepsy. Helping and loving her through her first seizure was a traumatic and shocking experience for me. From then on I began incorporating Conscious Grounding to help soothe her nervous system and keep calm during stressful events. I visualize a fun stack of dog treats, or her favorite toys connecting her body to the Earth. Now three years later her seizures do happen, but are mild and not very frequent. Considering her diagnosed condition, and prognosis from the neurologist, I am very pleased with the way Grounding has been helping manage her seizures.

Grounding Your Reproductive Organs

Every individual possesses both masculine and feminine energy, yet many struggle to distinguish their own gender energy from that of their parents or peers. People born with ovaries inherently carry a specific creative Divine Feminine energy that vibrates at a higher frequency. From an energetic perspective this energy is impossible to replicate by people born with testis. Grounding your reproductive organs facilitates the flow of this energy and facilitates the release of parental influences from this space.

Operating on parental energy is similar to using the wrong fuel in your car—it impedes your ability to function optimally. Grounding of ovaries allows individuals to release "male control energy" from external sources, freeing themselves from attempts to manipulate or dominate.

The opposite is also true. Foreign female energy in a male body often induces discomfort, resembling panic or anxiety due to its high vibrational frequency. Men typically resonate with slower, earthier vibrations and colors compared to women. By grounding the testicles and prostate, individuals can purge foreign female energy from their space and begin to separate from external male energy that may have previously influenced their sense of masculinity.

This Conscious Grounding process is done in connection to physical body and organs given at birth. It applies to all who have a physical body. You are honored in how you are identified as a spirit and as a person in the body. Release foreign energy so you can function most as Yourself.

To Ground your reproductive organs, visualize a Grounding cord and connect it to each of your ovaries or testis, as well as to left and right side of the sciatica nerve. Your grounding cord will have four anchor points. Drop it down to the center of the Earth as you do with your main Grounding cord, and flip it "on" to release foreign male or female energy from your body. This is also a great way to release pain from your legs and lower back.

Other suggestions of what you can ground for maximum benefit:

Job interview: Ground the room where you are interviewed and your resume. This will remove stuck energy and help you avoid having typing mistakes, or "accidentally" spilling water on the interviewer's laptop. Although you can not control the free will of the interviewer's decision making, you can ground negative influences that can prevent you from getting it, creating a neutral setting for you to shine your gifts.

Family gathering: while preparing for a family coming over for a gathering, ground your home using the technique described above. If you expect potentially charged dynamics, you can ground the table around which people are having dinner, ground the entrance door, and ground the couch where the family will gather after the meal. Create these "portals" so energy flair-ups have an opportunity to drain away.

This does not mean you are manipulating your family members' free will. Their choices, opinions, and political/religious viewpoints remain their own. You are creating Grounding for energy sparks to discharge, so instead of starting an emotional "fire," they dull and dissipate down the Grounding cords.

Things You Can Not Do with Your Grounding Cord

It is prudent to note a few things you can not control with the Grounding cord, such as winning the lottery, meddling with other people's free will, and death.

Grounding and $10,000

This is one of my favorite personal stories involving Grounding and neutrality. It was only some four or so years that I began openly talking about the spiritual practices in my self-care and beautification toolbox, while my experiences with them span almost three decades. This particular story begins with my PR trip to New York to promote a new product I was releasing through my brand, MAHALO Skin Care. A wonderful PR agency assembled a busy schedule of in-person visits to magazines, media, and beauty influencers.

November is always a very busy time in the business, so fitting in five days away was quite a stretch. Every step of the way, I grounded. I grounded my new product, my partner who stayed home to look after our new puppy, my team, myself, and my travel plans. The flight from Honolulu to New York is a red eye for 10 hours, landing me in the Big Apple at 9 am with a 6-hour jet lag. I went straight into conferences, meetings, and visits.

As both an energy practitioner and a conscious skincare founder, self-care is of top priority for me, so securing a first-class sleeper to allow me a reasonably good rest was a non-negotiable. The PR visits in New York were a dream. From spending time at the Condé Nast offices of Vogue, to GOOP and Forbes, I was reliving my own moments *ala* the Devil Wears Prada. Anna Wintour and Gwyneth Paltrow's beauty editors, and magazine prototypes were on the walls, and glamor, glamor, glamor. I fell in love with New York during that visit, and New York fell in love with my creations. Two days before departure, during our zig-zagging through Manhattan, I received a voicemail from United Airlines informing me they had an aircraft change for my return flight. They wondered if I would give up my first-class seat in exchange for a $600 credit. When I heard that message, I immediately grounded my reality. Knowing how exhausted I was and that I needed to sleep on the flight back, there was no option where I was not lying down to sleep on the return flight.

Once I was grounded, I let that topic out of my mind, continuing with the PR fun and New York. The night before my flight, I received another voicemail with the same request, now offering a $1000 credit in exchange for a seat. Again, ground, and let go. The morning of my flight, I stood in line to board the plane. It was 7 am, and I was exhausted. My only thought was sleep.

The flight crew made an announcement over the intercom repeating the story I had already heard twice: due to the change of aircraft, they did not have enough first-class seats and requested passengers to trade in their first-class ticket in exchange for a $1500 credit. I chuckle and remain unwavering in my knowingness of the need to lie down and sleep.

I ground this whole experience again. I ground the plane, the flight crew, and myself. I don't know how they will figure it out, but I know my Grounding cords are very strong, the energy is shifting, and all I have to do is to create the space for the opportunity to present itself.

After some kerfuffle with other passengers, I could finally board the plane, and it looked like I was the last unoccupied seat in first class. In my delight, I grabbed onto the pillow and absolutely beamed with excitement that in a few minutes, I could drift away into sleep. As I fussed around with my bags and the pillow, I heard the flight attendant asking first-class passengers to give up their seats, as they still had two more people waiting to board and must provide them with first-class seats.

As I sat on the chair, the flight attendant offered a $5000 credit in exchange for the seat. I remained seated, my body already mid-way into falling asleep.

My non-negotiable was unwavering: I needed to be lying down. The flight attendant's eyes locked with mine, and for some reason, he ignored all other passengers and spoke directly to me. His voice was begging. He said, "What if I offer you an entire middle row with four seats in our premium cabin so you can lie down, complimentary first-class food? You can keep your pillow and blanket and receive a $10,000 United flight credit." He paused and smiled nervously. All my needs AND more had been delivered. I said absolutely yes with gratitude and joy. What a miraculous experience, and shows how powerful this Grounding technique is.

I knew what I wanted. I cleared negative pain pictures related to bad travel stories with Airlines. I moved myself out of the way for the Universe to provide exactly what I needed and more. I remained in neutral. I grounded.

My life is filled with similar stories where circumstances, people, events, and even timelines shifted because I used the Grounding tool to clear stuck pain, clear pain blocks, connect to the source through Mother Earth, and remain in neutrality. I can't even begin to describe how often I hear, "We don't usually do this, but just this once for you." This is why I am so passionate about sharing this technique with you. It works.

AMUSEMENT BREAK

The other day I bought a Thesaurus, but when I got home and opened it, all the pages were blank.
I have no word to describe how angry I am.

Dealing with Grounding "Gremlins"

What To Do When Grounding is Difficult

Your first experiences with Grounding can be either euphoric or nothing at all. In most cases, however, they are quite beautiful, flowing, and validating. But as you continue to work on releasing the pain, you can hit edges of stuck energy that can activate discomfort, trigger you, cause you to cry, etc.

When Grounding consciously, your body releases pain that has come to the surface and is ready to be cleared. Some of that pain confetti could have been stuffed deep in your subconscious for a very long time.

As it comes up and out of your body, it can make its presence known, passing through with a last cry of anguish. ***Do not stop Grounding***. Remember you are safe. Whatever you are experiencing is just an echo, an emotional imprint, and not a real threat to your life. Let gravity take away the pain confetti; before you know it, you will feel relief and an expanded sensation of more space.

Try not to focus too much on the story or memory that might suddenly arise in your mind. If you experience a strong feeling or memory during your Grounding process, imagine turning those memories into colorful pieces of confetti and sending them swirling down the Grounding cord. As you allow the Grounding process to clear those energy blockages, you might realize that you can't remember what triggered you just a few minutes ago. By clearing the energy charge, you are removing your attachment to it.

Encouragement When Grounding is Difficult

It is worth reiterating how important it is to maintain the practice of Grounding, especially when you have a repelling desire against it. When you begin consciously Grounding pain confetti and proactively working to release energy blockages, you are bound to stir up the issues that kept you from facing them or Grounding in the first place.

When we looked at "fear" earlier, we highlighted two types of people: those who run toward fear and those who run away from it. Regardless of the category you might fall into, the practice of Grounding is your gateway toward freedom from pain and consequently from fear. Grounding is an exceptional opportunity to be in charge of the energies that prevent you from being happy, successful, healthy, or creating and living the life you want.

You have likely realized by now that no one is coming to save you despite the promises. So, is now a good time to end the course of your life that's not working for you? These Grounding techniques help you regain control over the obstacles and re-direct the course of your life on your terms.

Use Pleasure to Support You

Engaging in activities supporting your Grounding practice is another encouraging way to continue this practice, anything where your body can experience pleasure, feel good, and feel acknowledged and cared for. Skincare rituals are an excellent gateway to Grounding and becoming more present with the body. Beauty rituals like face masking followed by a massage, or MAHALO Skin Care's special "honey-rolling" technique will feed your body and mind. Involve yourself in various activities that bring you joy, as this alone will feed your spirit and assist your ability to be lovingly present and engaged in your daily life.

Nature is a sure way to replenish our life force and fill us with good feelings that inspire us to be more aligned with life. Nature and Grounding go hand in hand. Consider incorporating any of the following activities into your routine: hiking, biking, camping, gardening, dancing, painting, or doing anything that brings you immense pleasure.

Signs You Really Need to Ground

You blame others for your problems

When we redirect responsibility away from ourselves, it is a sure sign that a pain confetti has gained control over our emotions and minds. The horse blinders covering our wound are pain coming to the surface, ready to be released. This stagnant energy needs to go somewhere. If it is not released from the body, it gets redirected and used to judge others.

The wisdom in us can recognize that whatever we point the finger at in the other, is actually a pain lighting up inside us. This is a perfect scenario when Grounding to release pain confetti can liberate you from layers of personal and generational pain.

You don't hear your intuition

The times when you find yourself indecisive, feeling stuck, unable to hear yourself, confused, or overwhelmed create a wonderful opportunity to Ground and clear emotional blocks that prevent you from experiencing your full range of emotions and energy flow. This can actually become your reminder to ground. Notice that something is out of alignment in your life, in how you perceive things, or you cannot make a clear choice or course of action. Allow yourself 15-20 minutes of Conscious Grounding to shift the energy, reconnect yourself with the Earth, clear pain, and regain your clarity.

You compare yourself to others

Comparison is another valuable sign that you are operating with a *confetti* of unworthiness. Be amused when you begin to compare. Be excited (or try to, as much as you can) that you were able to stir up this confetti and bring it to the surface. When you feel the negative competition chatter inside yourself, and the nagging talk of "the other is better than me" gets stuck in your head, catch yourself, sit down, and ground.

Allow this energy to find an outlet and release from your body. What's the worst that can happen, anyway? You "lose" 15 minutes of your day and give yourself the gift of personal attention. If the competition thought is true, it will still be there after you complete a 15-minute Grounding practice.

You are sulking in feeling victimized

Although it can feel quite enjoyable, feeling sorry for yourself accomplishes absolutely nothing. Moreover, it keeps you stuck and in more pain. This type of addictive behavior is nothing more than a distraction from your own freedom and personal self-discovery.

Being stuck in victimhood is a coping mechanism from a traumatic experience when we disassociate from facing that pain. But by doing so, we also disassociate from the source of personal power, freedom, and the ability to create circumstances we actually want. So many of these stuck behaviors are a catch-22 and require your active participation to disconnect from them.

Once again, take charge of your happiness, learn Grounding processes, and claim your personal freedom.

You feel resentment

Resentment toward others, toward yourself, and toward unfair situations will keep you stuck in places in life where there is no growth, no joy, no flow of energy, and places you don't want to be. Comparing yourself to others, beating up on yourself, and not taking accountability for your role in situations will never heal the pain. They only beget more negativity in your life and keep you stuck, looping in the same familiar pain over and over.

Other situations that call to ground:

If you feel depression or apathy for longer than a fleeting moment, Ground.

During the onset of an illness such as a cold or flu. Ground.

At bedtime, before going to sleep, Ground yourself, your bed, and your home.

When you feel vulnerable, spacey, forgetful, clumsy, Ground for clarity.

Before a big meeting, presentation, or a lecture. Ground.

When working with electronics, Ground yourself and the equipment.

When you feel disconnected from reality and the people around you. Ground for connection.

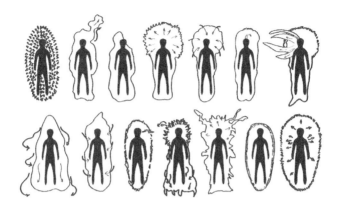

The Aura

Everything, including the Universe itself, has a vibration. These vibrations fluctuate similarly to musical notes from high to low, but this does not necessarily mean that low is bad or high is good. Universal intelligence makes no such polarizing distinctions and the notion of good/bad and light/dark is a part of the human experience. From the Universal perspective, things "are" as they are.

Vibrations can be faster or slower, higher or lower, quieter or louder, etc. The strength and length of these vibrations create a bubble around whatever emits that vibration. Humans, ants, plants, and planet Earth all emit their own vibrations, each with their own pitch, pulse, strength, and length. The edges create their individual bubbles.

Aura is Our Own Personal Universe

In Eastern traditions, this bioplasmic bubble is called *Pranamaya Kosha* and is believed to be experienced by every living and conscious being. It is understood as the vital energy, breath, or sheath of life force.

In Sanskrit, the word *Prana* refers to life force and is the word for breath. More commonly, these vibrations are referred to as Auras, and Aura bubbles, and are viewed as an energy field that surrounds your body. The Aura changes color and size with emotions. A technique known as muscle-testing demonstrates the energy changes accompanying emotions, as our body's muscles instantly respond to positive and negative stimuli.

In this guide, we will look at an Aura bubble as a storage containing all information about our reality, traumas, beliefs, etc. The Ākāśa records are accessed through the Aura layers. As our basic emotional states transmit themselves to the universe, our Aura bubble is our personal universe.

Seeing & Sensing the Aura

Many ancient cultures hold the concept of Aura at the core of their traditions. Although modern science has attempted to disprove this notion, researchers in Spain were able to ascertain that although actual evidence of Auras has not been proven (or disproven), the ability for some people to see the Aura is due to the neuropsychological phenomenon known as "synesthesia" (specifically, "emotional synesthesia").

People with "synesthesia" can see the Aura around people, objects, trees, and so forth. For others, without this naturally-born ability, "seeing" an Aura is done through meditative visualization, like the one we use for our Grounding practice. The edge of your Aura has an electric blue color, which makes it easier to *see* with more familiarized practice. Since Aura is simply an edge of a vibration, it can be expanded to be as big as the room you are in, contracted extremely close to the body, and be moved around in front, behind, or off to the side.

Your Aura bubble's balanced vibrational length, with an Aura edge evenly distributed about two feet around the body, is usually more comfortable for you and those around you. Grounding the Aura bubble and each layer within, which we will explore later in this chapter, helps achieve this.

Aura Does Not Lie

Whether you are a person who can "see" Aura or not, all of us have a varied degree of sensing Auras. A good example is when we feel comfortable around some people while finding others intolerable. Aura does not lie; it is the quality of the sum effect of all elements of the person. All aspects that make them an individual - emotional, mental, physical, religious, social, cultural, spiritual facets, as well as the beliefs, traumas, and pain that are stored within. Add all the past life experiences and their layers of mental, physical, and religious facets. All this makes Auras a complex and "high tech" information storage.

For this reason, people suffering from negative ideas, thoughts, and energies can feel draining to those who come in contact with them. Here, the fundamental "Law of Nature" comes into play. The energy flows from the higher concentration area to the lower concentration area. You can feel wonderful one moment, be approached by someone operating at a lower energetic concentration, and suddenly feel agitated, moody, or sad. (*This is the perfect time to Ground.*)

However, this does not mean we are victims of the "Law of Nature" circumstances or that to protect ourselves from being affected by those at lower concentrations, we need to lock ourselves in the house and never interact with anyone. Grounding practice is your most potent "defense" against "Aura drainers."

By connecting yourself to the Earth, you are activating the gravity shoot that simply drains away whatever "lower concentration" energies you come in contact with. And, what's better, you also clear your own emotional pain confetti that got magnetized in the mix.

Keeping Your Aura Protected

/ / David was returning from his yoga class, cheerfully waiting by the elevator, humming a tune from his favorite song. He was enjoying the endorphins released by his body from exercise and excited about a delicious acai bowl he picked up on the way home. As the elevator doors were about to close, his neighbor jumped inside, all frantic and disheveled, looking for the keys in her purse. "You were playing music loudly last night when you knew the cut-off was at 10 pm", she said. Without letting him say a word, she continued, "I wasn't able to fall asleep, and because of that, I was late to my morning doctor's appointment."

She went on and on, sharing the zig zags of her days. As David stood there, he observed within himself first a cloud of guilt that came over him, even though he knew that he turned the music off at 10:07, or that he personally had nothing to do with the reason his neighbor couldn't sleep. He realized that her stories, her behavior and the way she seemingly blamed him for her misfortunes of that day reminded him of his father.

His dad was a professor at a local college, divorced, raising a gay son. The guilt of the loss of his marriage and the shame of his "not normal" son not turning out the way society expected has made David's father blame David for all things wrong in the world. However, as a practiced grounding practitioner, David recognized this pattern from the moment his neighbor began to speak. Before the elevator door had the chance to close, he created a new Grounding cord for himself, one for his neighbor, and one for the elevator. As he turned on the gravity and released, he recognized how the lower energy vibrations of his neighbor tried to pull and sort of "vampire" happy energy vibrations from him.

His Grounding cord did the job of draining away any tugs, pulls, or attempts to take energy from him. Plus, more of the pain confetti from the memories of his father were able to come to the surface, magnetized by the matching frequency of his neighbor, allowing him to free himself from more pain. All of that in one elevator ride. He was able to remain unfazed and help his neighbor neutralize her energetic attack.

The Wonders of a Healer's Aura

This "Law of Nature," when used by people who have mastered working with the energies, can bring wonders. Sick people get healed in the presence of accomplished healers.

Since the Aura is simply the outer edge of a vibrational frequency, it is said that some healers have an Aura as big as 10-20 miles. Anyone within 10-20 miles of this healer would become nonviolent. The awareness and mastery of your *Kosha* / sheath / Aura bubble allow you to move stagnant energy, allowing you to experience greater vitality and an energetic connection to yourself, others, and nature.

Different Perspectives on Aura

Attributing each Aura layer with a particular color has been popularized, implying an underlying connotation of bad, better, or good. This guide approaches colors in Aura layers from a neutral perspective without giving them any such labels.

There is wisdom, information, and purpose in all colors. When used with a Grounding cord to release pain, colors released from energy centers and Auras simply carry a particular vibration of stuck *confetti*: pain, shame, blame, heartbreak, insecurity etc.

For the purpose of this guide, we will explore seven main Aura layers, and the type of pain confetti stored in each. These may differ from colors assigned to certain aura layers in other training.

1st Survival Aura Layer

This layer is positioned closest to our body and stores information related to survival. Vibrations from this Aura layer have the most dense frequency and the slowest oscillating wave. In this layer, we process and store all information and emotions associated with money, health, survival, and body safety. Emotional pain related to not having enough or working hard to survive is found as pain confetti scattered in this Aura layer.

We often see family lineage karma (*energy patterns*) stuck in this Aura layer, associated with lack. Even if a person has financial means, a good job, and so forth, this type of stuck energy will continue to activate thought patterns, limiting beliefs, and nagging thoughts that push a person to work harder and constantly worry about not having enough.

This can manifest physically as sciatica, leg and leg joint pain, eating disorders, reproductive issues, insomnia or excessive sleeping, colon or bladder issues, lower back pain, insecurity, anxiety, lack of direction, depression, apathy, and disassociating.

2nd Emotions and Sexuality Aura Layer

This Aura layer often holds stored *pain confetti* related to our sexuality, desires, and early experiences with our caregivers. In male bodies, stuck emotional *pain confetti* related to their mothers is found in this layer. Or if their father was not emotionally warm and caring, the person would stuff their need for male validation and desire for fatherly love as a stuck emotional pain in this level.

Men who have trouble expressing their emotions, are unable to express their feelings, show affection as tough love, refuse to go to therapy, and believe they are absolutely fine usually have stuck emotional *pain confetti* scattered all over this Aura layer. Similarly, for women, painful emotions relating to their father are found in this layer. This Aura layer is especially important for people with female bodies, as it is the energetic layer of creation.

When the second Aura layer is clear of stuck emotional pain, we can have more fulfilling relationships, rich intimacy, and enjoy the physical elements of life, such as pleasure.

Stored emotional pain and energy blockages in the 2nd Aura layer show up as issues with the reproductive system. Physical manifestations of stuck energy in this layer: reproductive system illness, hip issues, spleen and kidney problems, PMS, arthritis, and anemia.

3rd Dreams Aura Layer

How you integrate your spiritual experiences into your physical and daily life gets stored in this layer. Defining spiritual experience is fully personal. It can be anything from communing with Greater Consciousness, walking in the forest, or admiring art. As the expression goes, "Beauty is in the Eyes of the Beholder."

The third Aura layer stores information our subconscious mind receives but isn't fully integrated or seen by our conscious mind. Unprocessed information from this Aura layer often shows up in our dreams.

Stuck emotional pain in the third layer manifests in our physical body as hormonal system dysfunctions, lower back pain, and GI issues.

4th Affinity Aura Layer

Not to be confused with the heart chakra, the fourth Aura layer stores information related to self-love, self-worth, and affinity.

Energy frequencies begin to become higher and more pulsating from this layer on. The Layer of Affinity is often seen as a gateway to a person's manifestation potential. The easier the flow of the frequency is within this layer, the easier it is to attract everything and anything we need, and desire.

Physical manifestations of stuck pain in this Aura layer are related to the chest, lungs, middle and upper back, and blood.

5th Creativity and Communication Aura Layer

This Aura layer has the potential to create change. All impactful speeches, works of art, and soul-touching creativity are produced from this Aura layer. When functioning at its ultimate, it has the ability to invoke the pure essence of truth, delivered with kindness and neutrality.

In our practice, this Aura layer is often one of the most blocked and energetically charged with stuck *pain confetti*. Not being allowed to speak your truth, or expressing truth with anger or harm causes energetic blockages in this Aura layer.

Physical ailments often manifest as autoimmune disease, thyroid, and hormonal imbalances.

6th Conscious Awareness Aura Layer

This Aura layer is primarily connected to the pineal gland and cerebral cortex. If you have ever wondered if you are crazy for "seeing" or sensing that "6th sense" energy, you might not be crazy but clairvoyant. You possess an ability of "clear vision" or conscious awareness. Since every human has this 6th Aura layer, we all have clairvoyant, or "6th sense" abilities.

Stuck energy in this Aura layer shows up as mental disorders, sometimes as severe as schizophrenia, or as lightly as nervousness and antisocial tendencies.

7th Spirit Personality Aura Layer

The highest vibrational frequency described by the Taittiriya Upanishad (The Vedic Ancient Wisdom II.2.6) gives this Aura layer the vibrational power of 1000 petals. An enlightened soul with a fully purified 7th Aura layer exhibits the maximum Aura vibration. This person has the capacity to impact others within a 10-20 mile radius to become non-violent. Known examples are Buddha, Jesus Christ, Mary Magdalene, and others.

Stuck emotional pain related to dogmatic, organized religions, and prosecution to your freedom is often found in this Aura layer. Clearing it by Grounding this Aura layer brings you one step closer to that of Buddha and Christ consciousness.

Grounding Your Aura Bubble

Despite sounding complex and ancient, working with Aura layers for the purposes of our play (*remember the kindergarten approach you were invited to take with this guide?*) is actually very easy. Once you have become accustomed and comfortable with incorporating conscious Grounding using the main practice, you have the option to add a few more additions to it. As with the main Grounding practice, this can be done anytime, anywhere. The process, *you guessed it*, is simple:

B egin by getting your body grounded as described on page 63 and releasing pain.

S tay in the Grounding practice for as long as you need.

F eel the gravity draining the stuck energy that has come to the surface and is ready to leave your body.

U sing the same visualization technique, "see" an electric blue edge around your body. Your "seeing" can be anything from actually seeing the flickering edge of blue light, to sensing an energetic ending of "you" to simply knowing it is there.

You may hear a slight energetic murmur, or some people can smell the edge of the Aura (*I have heard it described as "freshly broken twig of willow"*). Or if none of those is your way, then why not play pretend like kids do in kindergarten and draw yourself a "line in the sand" with blue crayon and call it "mine," my Aura?

Notice how far or how close to the body your Aura is today. Is it all the way outside of your room, or is it tightly snug around your body like an 80s workout outfit?

Adjust your Aura to be about two feet around your body. Play with it. If it is close to you, bring the palms of your hands close to your body, facing out, and then slowly push outside when you reach two feet from you. If it is too far, then spread your arms out, palms facing in, and bring the palms towards you until they reach two feet from you. How does this feel?

Visualize the outer edge of your Aura bubble tucking into your Grounding cord. Attach it under your feet like you are tucking in a shirt.

Visualize a switch, and turn it "on" to release the outer edge of your Aura bubble.

Grounding Each Aura Layer

Follow the same steps to ground each Aura layer individually, adding a conscious attention to each Aura layer. It will look as follows:

B egin by Grounding your body by visualizing the Grounding cord and connecting it at the bottom of the first energy center, near the coccygeal plexus (pelvic area), and connecting it with the core of the Earth.

V isualize the switch in front of you and flip it "on" to release. Let the Earth's gravity take away the pain confetti ready to release.

S ee" your Aura bubble. Notice how far or close it is to your body. Bring it to be about two feet away from your body.

B egin to ground each individual Aura layer, tucking them into the Grounding cord one by one (see drawing on the next page)

    1st layer: survival
    2nd layer: emotions & sexuality
    3rd layer: dreams & subconscious
    4th layer: affinity
    5th layer: creativity & communication
    6th layer: conscious awareness
    7th layer: spirit personality

Visualize a switch and flip it "on" to release each of the Aura layers

You are now mastering the ultimate level of freeing yourself from pain, creating space, and claiming your freedom.

7 aura layers

Grounding Cord

NOTES & OBSERVATIONS

Other People's Energy

Is It You, Or Is It Them?

Grounding is a practice that keeps on giving. As you continue with your practice, you begin to familiarize yourself with the sound, tone, vibration, and feeling of your energy. In simpler terms, you begin to know yourself and what it is like being you. The more *pain confetti* you clear from your energy body, the more solid your connection to self becomes.

As was shared in an example of AM/FM frequencies earlier, a person who does not practice Grounding often carries within their emotional, physical, and mental energies not only the array of their own pain confetti but also a cacophony of other people's emotions, thoughts and projections. Pain confetti likes company; when not moved from the body, it expands and multiplies.

With this cacophony of noise inside, hearing one's authentic voice is similar to listening to the early AM MONO radio. The transmission pops, crackles, frizzles, and is often interjected by a different radio station. One moment, you are listening to a happy song; the next second, a grouchy voice comes in telling you about a snowstorm in Wisconsin.

So how do you decide: is it you, or is it them? Grounding, of course. Release, release, release the pain and energy blocks that prevent you from hearing your voice. The more you clear, the clearer the sound gets.

What Do You Sound Like?

Another way to identify if you hold another person's energy in your body is to know how your energy feels in your body—your own flavor. Once again, this is done by gradually releasing stuck pain, the *pain confetti*.

As you clear stuck emotions, the static clears and you begin to hear the sound in a clear quality of an FM stereo. Your energy is clearer, safe, nurturing, and supportive. If you then start to feel confused in your own thoughts, having unclear, jumbled feelings or ideas, when the sound is no longer an FM, that is a good indication that you might be picking-up, or consciously taking on other people's energies in your space.

Picking up other people's energies is unavoidable. As compassionate, empathic beings, the need for connection drives us. The difference is how much of the "handling" of that energy you take upon yourself.

First, you can simply notice the difference in your body. Recognize where your own frequency ends and another begins. If you have difficulty finding that distinction, a 10- to 15-minute Grounding practice of the Aura layers will help shift your perspective.

Ask yourself: Is the other person trying to solve their problems through me? Can I solve this problem for them? Is it my responsibility to solve this problem for them? (Hint: the answer to the last two questions is NO.)

When you start looking at this from a grounded perspective of neutrality, you will likely notice that someone else's problem creates frustration in your space and may even cause feelings of hopelessness and confusion.

It's Not Your Problem

Once you are clear that a thought or feeling is not yours, you can easily Ground it from your body. As you ground, you can test this by asking if that same thought lingers in your mind or if the feeling still triggers you. If it has disappeared, see it as another validating confirmation that you recognized someone else's energy in your body and moved it out of your system.

This "skill" is especially valuable in our modern civilization. Besides our loved ones, neighbors, or people on the street who try to process their problems through us (projection), we are also being bombarded by marketing, social media, and politics, infusing our energy space with their agenda, problems, and need to control us. When we are not in a grounded state of neutrality, we buy into their propaganda by believing their foreign frequency in our body is our frequency. We confuse "their truth" for "our truth."

This is not to say that we need to disagree with everything and everyone. On the contrary, this is to say that we remain whole and complete within our own truth, neutrality, and connection to our source, Earth's energy. Whatever resonates with our truth does as it does. What does not will simply bounce off. We remain unaffected and unfazed by triggers, rhetoric, marketing ploys, or manipulation. Other people's problems will not stick to you when you are Grounded.

Grounding stays part of your body for 24-48 hours. When someone tries to hook you with their problems, they will just slide down your Grounding cord.

Golden Sun & Self Healing

For the "dessert" of this experiential guide, we have a very special tool that pairs beautifully with your Grounding practice. As you master the process of releasing *pain confetti* from your physical, emotional, and mental bodies, you free space that was occupied by pain or other people's energies. That space is now yours to fill with whatever you want or need. The following tool does exactly that.

Similarly, as you can never have enough Grounding, you can never have enough Golden Suns. A Golden Sun is a visualized mental image that allows you to collect your spiritual energy from various people, places, and things and give it back to your body. Your spiritual energy, the gold energy that fills your Golden Sun, is made up of various vibrations, including (but not limited to) your healing energy, creative energy, vitality, awareness, etc.

Don't Miss This Step

Nourishing and filling yourself with the Golden Sun is an important part of Grounding. When you release the stuck energy in your body, you create space once occupied by pain, and other people's energy.

The human body doesn't deal well with emptiness. In truth, it would rather have the old issues in there rather than nothing at all. That space needs to be filled with something.

If left vacant, it will likely be filled by other *pain confetti,* or re-attract those old situations back into your life and re-create more of the pain you have just released. Therefore, after you Ground, always remember to fill the space with NEW energy you want. Be very generous here; there is an abundant supply of sun and positive vibrations for the taking.

As the old issues and pain leave your body, you come to a point where you have a choice of what you want to have. Fill your body with new information, new feelings, new vibrations of being truly connected and integrated as a whole human being on every level of your intentions. Remember the concept of kindergarten here.

Reach your arms out into the Universe and say MINE! This positive energy is mine, and I want all of it.

Using Golden Sun to Collect Yourself Back

This tool is used with the Grounding practice. Once you have grounded yourself, your Aura layers, and perhaps the room in which you meditate, you can begin to work the Golden Sun tool.

C reate (visualize) a mental image picture of a large Gold Bubble over your head.

C reate (visualize) a magnet and throw it in the middle of that Gold Bubble. Allow the magnet to attract and collect all of your spiritual energy, then call it back into the bubble.

A llow the Golden Sun to fill up with your energy and get full, big, and bright.

O nce full, purify this bubble of any unwanted or foreign energy that might have snuck in. To purify, visualize creative fire under that bubble, seeing it boil and get as hot as the actual Sun to burn away any energy that is not yours.

O *ptional*: In addition to gathering your energy, you can add boiling bubbles, flavors, or rainbow colors of any energy you would like to bring into your body (*amusement, certainty, prosperity, joy, answers, validation, etc*). It's similar to doing affirmations but 1000 times more powerful.

V isualize poking a hole at the bottom of the Golden Sun bubble and allow all the energy to pour into your body. Visualize it pouring from the top of your head into every cell of your body, down to the tips of your fingers and toes.

R epeat this process by bringing in as many Golden Suns as needed to feel nourished and refreshed.

Things You Can Do With the Golden Sun

Similar to how we have explored various options for applying Grounding, you can enhance your energy experiences by adding replenishments with the Golden Sun.

Golden Sun in Your House

After Grounding your house using the process described above, visualize a gold bubble above your room, or entire house. Toss a magnet inside that bubble and pour in the flavor of energy you want to experience in your home: *harmony, joy, love, prosperity, calmness, health, etc.*

Visualize the bubble above your house filling up. Make it big, as big as you are comfortable imagining. When it is full, bring it to a boil, making it as hot as the sun itself. Purify to remove any unwanted energy. Poke a hole at the bottom of the bubble, let the Golden Sun empty, and fill your entire house with the golden vibration of the energy you'd like to bring into your home.

Collecting Back Your Energy

When we come in contact with people, whether through intimate interactions with our family or insignificant encounters like being complimented by a stranger, bits of our energy get left behind with each interaction. Each person, and even every element our senses engage with—such as sights our eyes perceive or sounds our ears hear—a small imprint of our energy is left behind, similar to the fingerprints we leave on objects we touch.

Conscious Grounding helps you free yourself from other people's energy in your space, clear your stuck emotional pain, and connect you with the Earth to Ground unwanted energetic cause and effect. The Golden Sun tool helps you collect back your energy, fill yourself with your own frequency, and add more of what you actually want to experience and create in your life.

It is a valuable practice to collect your energy using the Golden Sun tool at the end of every day. Collect yourself back from every place, connection, interaction, or experience you've had. All the little fragments of your energy left scattered around leave you feeling incomplete, frazzled, and often empty.

Follow the above process of collecting your energy back using the Golden Sun tool.

The Results from Grounding

The most obvious and observable results of Grounding and clearing the *pain confetti* are resolutions of long-standing issues, and challenges, as well as the resurgence in mental, emotional, and spiritual capacity and growth. As we continue to experience the nourishing benefits of removing barriers to fulfillment in life, the space previously filled by suffering, limitations, physical ailments, and fear gets replaced by more and more pleasure and satisfaction. A realization emerges that the negative thoughts and beliefs we held as truth were merely the consequence of accumulated stuck pain. We go from seeking external validation to having an unwavering sense of inner knowing, self-assurance, trust, and self-validation. What used to seem impossibly difficult can become effortless and vibrantly thriving.

Problem Solving

Using Grounding for problem solving is a wonderful way to get results, while simultaneously clearing the energetic blockages that might have created the problem in the first place. The angle from which Grounding approaches problem solving is neutrality, and once again, kindergarten. Rather than seeking how to fix the problem, one releases the emotions that drive the inquiry.

Instead of forcing the mind to seek the answers, use the mind to connect your body and its energy field to that of the Earth and let gravity take away the charge that is blinding one to seeing the solution.

When the frazzled energy, chaos and *pain confetti*, external influence, invalidation and other obstacles drain from our system through Grounding, the answer will be there waiting for us. We will not have to look for it.

Consider how effortless and easy this is compared to the mind's typical prolonged, overcomplicated ways to problem solve. The mind is overworking because it is overburdened by layers and layers of stuck emotional pain confetti obstructing the clear flow of energy and communication.

Grounding & Therapy

Broadly speaking, Grounding is a much more accessible, and free of charge practice that can deliver quicker tangible results than therapy, offering a more freeing and stimulating path to expanding consciousness and awareness. While therapy excels in unveiling patterns that can be distilled into words, stories, and exact definitions, the integration of both practices can accelerate and enhance the overarching goals.

Therapy has an appeal for its greater intellectual satisfaction due to its verbal nature and emphasis on understanding the reason behind a given behavior, the *"why."* However, this intellectual focus can also be a limitation, as it often results in merely gaining insight without addressing the full process of handling the emotions—mentally, physically, and energetically.

Emotional work in therapy can also be slow, uncomfortable, and often avoided altogether. In contrast, Grounding prioritizes the emotional clearing in each moment, bypassing intellectual analysis and focusing directly on releasing emotional pain, the *"what."*

By releasing the *pain confetti* that created a given behavior, the *"why"* naturally clears once the *"what"* has been discharged and released from our physical, mental, and emotional bodies. When we engage in the process of Conscious Grounding, we often don't even have to think, or process what *pain confetti* is ready to be released.

The need to analyze, digest, rehash, and talk through every nuance of a traumatic experience is replaced by simply allowing those "pain picture" energies to leave our body and go down the Grounding cord with the help of the Earth's gravitational pull. Freedom from depression doesn't necessarily require probing its underlying causes; rather, it entails releasing oneself from its grip in the present moment.

The goal of Grounding is to free oneself from the fundamental source of all suffering and pain.

A Change in Trajectory

While grounding may indeed be simple and effortless, its ultimate impact is remarkably profound. Using the mind to visualize the release of emotional pain, done with amusement, and child-like wonder, often leads to significant change and impact.

"If you think you are too small to make a difference, try sleeping with a mosquito"—one of my favorite quotes by the Dalai Lama, and is so perfectly applicable to Grounding. The Grounding practice is that tiny little

adjustment, that one percent modification, that one-degree shift in a ship's compass that over time leads to a very different destination from the original course. Shifting from operating based on beliefs of lack driven by stuck emotional pain, to now operating from freedom of space filled with possibilities, expansion, joy, and self-trust.

Impact on Health

The average person is often consumed by concerns regarding the body—its function, performance, appearance, and basic survival. Similarly, the average mind is overwhelmed with anxieties and fears of illness, suffering, and death, pushing the mind to defend the body through various means then. The internal tension of excessive focus on diet, weight management, physical activity, and the health of the environment often leaves the person feeling depleted, drained, and fatigued. This can leave one feeling like a victim of circumstances.

Notice how much energy is required to support this constant preoccupation with fears and worries. Since the body obeys the mind, and the mind is the manifestation tool by which awareness and cognition take form, these preoccupations are merely the product of the mind, with the body reacting to them.

As we engage in the Conscious Grounding practice to release all the *pain confetti* of mind-created stuck energy patterns, we free ourselves from these belief systems. We create more space for freedom and move into a more vital state of health, wellness, and life-force energy.

As we Ground-out the endless variety of blockages stuck in the body, fear, concerns, and negative belief systems through clearing *pain confetti*, many physical illnesses begin to resolve automatically. The body begins to function effortlessly, smoothly, and with no obsession over health.

A grounded person is no longer subject to fear of pollutants, germs, electromagnetic frequencies, pollen, dust, and other contaminants. The more you clear the emotional pain that causes illness like autoimmune disease, the fewer physical manifestations of ailments will be present in the body. By Grounding emotional pain, you do, indeed, heal yourself. Many diseases can be reversed unless there is a strong karmic dominance to the contrary.

AMUSEMENT BREAK

Did you hear about the guy who went to the doctor for a headache? The doctor examined his ear and found money. The doctor kept pulling and pulling money out until he had $1,999. Then the doctor said, "No wonder you're not feeling two grand!"

I made a song about tortilla once, now it's more like a wrap.

Grounding & Beauty Rituals

In my 15+ years of working in the beauty industry and especially through my own skin care brand, I have had the opportunity to intimately connect with many people. In this safe, personal space of connecting through skin care, beauty becomes a catalyst for many women (and men) to share their life stories, challenges, and questions, and to seek deeper connection both with others and themselves. It can also be a source of great pain and much *confetti*.

My confidential folder is filled with heartfelt client correspondence whose lives have been transformed by re-connecting to their beauty rituals through Conscious Grounding practice, accessing their sacred beauty through skin, and spirit. They use Grounding as part of their beauty and skin care rituals to gain sovereignty over their self-criticism, narcissistic attachments, anxiety, and physical manifestations of stuck emotional pain.

I've witnessed stories of so many women whose stuck pain manifested as reproductive organ illness, such as PCOS, infertility, and fibroids. The negative and toxic pain confetti repeats and amplifies the negative self-affirming beliefs of fat, ugly, unlovable, too many wrinkles, awkward, not good enough, too much, not enough, etc etc. The resulting numbness of their creative energy flow blocks their access to vital life force and beauty within them.

Skin care routines can be profoundly satisfactory. Social media is ample with accounts with multiple millions of followers and viewership centered around make-up, cleansing, facial massage, or the latest discovery in skin care. It is a potent boost of dopamine, that provides an incredible opportunity, a gateway for connecting deeper into oneself.

The touch of our own hands to skin makes the brain release endorphins and pleasure hormones, boosting happiness and validation—truly wonderful things. This boost of happy chemicals is an ideal time to connect with oneself in a playful and abundant way to harness all the potential for self-empowering self-love.

Combined with the practice of Grounding, when a person engages their connection, and attention to their body through the act of self-love in a skin care ritual, and allows for a Conscious Grounding release of pain, they create space, freedom, and lasting impact. This rewires both the brain towards an unconscious habit of routine cleansing or make-up to now a ritual of rekindled self-love, honoring our whole beauty, creating reconnection with their true sacred Self.

Self-acceptance, love of our curves, confidence, healthy relationships, glowing skin, unshakable self-esteem, and grace are born from Grounding and Beauty Rituals.

Skin • Spirit • Sacred

Discover more about MAHALO Skin Care
www.mahalo.care

Grounding & Sacred Land

Over the past twenty-plus years, I have been blessed with opportunities to travel and commune with sacred lands around the world. From trekking the Himalayas, ancient caves in Tibet, and energetic vortexes in Sedona, to manifesting incredible experiences like spending an hour completely alone inside the Pyramid of Giza, or a solo meditation at midnight in the center of Stonehenge during the rising of a full moon. Mount Shasta, Glastonbury, Chitchen Itza, Puri, Santiago De Compostela, Isle of Iona, Haleakala, Lourdes, Jerusalem, Varanasi, Haida Gwaii, Vatican, Thingvellir, Petra, Redwood Forests, Rila Monastery, Taj Mahal, Luxor, Annapurna, and more. I have visited many of the energy vortexes and their ley lines, chakras or energy centers of the planet, and places of spiritual or religious significance.

Through the years of traveling, returning to, or making a pilgrimage to these places around the world, I began to deepen my connection and relationship to the Earth, her vibrational frequencies, learning and understanding her ways. Each sacred, or energetically significant area of land helped me rekindle and strengthen my love affair with Mother Earth.

Being in communion with each sacred or significant land, I discovered that by consciously engaging with the energy vibration of the area, I am able to tap into and unlock the sacred codes of wisdom, awareness, and what many refer to as mysteries. The Grounding practice in the sacred land takes a whole deeper meaning and a form of not simply clearing me from pain, but unifying my physical and spiritual bodies with that of the Earth, opening the doors to the Divine in my heart.

With time, I also began to realize that one does not have to physically travel to any of these sacred places to tap into their energies in the present moment. When used together with Grounding, the Golden Sun tool is the easiest way to collect, and call to yourself the frequencies of any of the chakras/energy centers of the Earth, or to fill yourself with the vibrations of the Sedona vortexes.

Simply visualize calling that frequency into your Golden Sun, purify it by boiling it to match the heat and vibrancy of the sun itself, and bring it into your body. As you are connected to the Earth through the Grounding cord, attuning to Earth's sacred land through no time, no space is a potent energy practice of raising your vibrational frequency.

Connect to the Heart Chakra of the Earth

Give it a try. Set aside 15-20 minutes for Conscious Grounding and Sacred Land connection. Ground yourself. Allow Earth's gravity to clear layers of pain that are ready for release—grow and Ground your seven Aura layers. Create a Golden Sun bubble over your head, toss a magnet inside it, and visualize the sacred land you want to attune to. How about Glastonbury, the heart chakra of the Earth? Call in the vibrational frequencies of the mystical isle of Avalon that is Glastonbury to fill your Golden Sun. Call in vibrations of embodied unconditional love, affinity, and all the flavors associated with the heart. That sacred land holds all those vibrations within her. Call them into your Golden Sun, purify it, and bring it into your body.

Helpful Tip:

To help you connect with Sacred Land, you can search online for photos, videos, and descriptions of the land. This will help you visualize and call in the vibrations of that land.

To make this even more potent, look up the history of the most abundant time period for that region. This will give you an opportunity to tune into that sacred land at its most energetically potent time. For example, the early 1500s (period of famed Tudor king Henry VIII) were peak years in Glastonbury, when it was the wealthiest and most powerful in England's network of Abbeys, owning a quarter of all English land and having four times the income of the king. In your visualization meditation, you can call in the vibration frequencies of Glastonbury from those years. Imagine what it looked like back then, what clothes people wore, and what kind of music, food, or art was enjoyed in affinity and abundance. Tune your physical and energetic body to the highest frequency of the sacred land, and that land's height of power by using the Grounding, and Golden Sun tools.

***Enjoy your freedom, and
endless possibilities.***

Earth's Energy Centers (Chakras)

Mount Shasta, USA (Root Chakra)
Lake Titicaca, Peru (Sacral Chakra)
Uluru, AUS (Solar Plexus Chakra)
Glastonbury, UK (Heart Chakra)
Pyramid of Giza, Egypt (Throat Chakra)
Shaftesbury to Stonehenge, UK (Third Eye Chakra)
Kailash, Tibet (Crown Chakra) is inaccessible, but it is
a place we travel to in meditation

Experience the Skin • Spirit • Sacred

by joining Merina and Global Guest Teachers
on our retreats, journeys and events

Stay connected:

www.mahalo.care

www.mahalo.care/events/

www.mahalo.care/podcast/

www.instagram.com/mahalo.care/

Frequently Asked Questions

Q: *Do I have to ground every day?*

In the beginning, and for a while, yes.

Create a habit about your Grounding practice. Wake up five minutes before you normally begin your day by Grounding while still in bed. Ground yourself, and the day ahead of you. Ground a few times throughout the day, anytime, anywhere. You can ground while doing the dishes, driving, watching a movie, or in a dedicated 15-20 minute seated meditation (most ideal).

Make Grounding a part of your everyday practice.

Choose an object, a scent, or an art form that you bring as part of your Grounding practice. Train your mind to connect that scent/object with your Grounding practice. It will then act as a catalyst to remind you to ground and how good it feels in your body when you ground and meditate.

Q: *I have been Grounding for a while, surely I should be free of the pain you mention, but some days I feel worse.*

Yes, the feelings of pain will eventually fade away. As you continue with the Grounding process, you will free yourself from more and more of those energetic blockages, feeling significantly lighter and more at ease.

There may be moments when you wonder how long this will continue and whether it will ever end. Rest assured, it will, and every aspect of your life will greatly improve.

Q: *I am unable to feel the Grounding flow as explained in this guide. I don't feel the energy. Why is that?*

When we are unable to feel the Grounding, it is a great indication that there are some energy blockages in the lower energy centers of the body that prevent the flow of energy and block our ability to feel. Lower parts of our body store a multitude of information related to survival.

Your body and mind are likely protecting you from re-experiencing old traumas by numbing or blocking the energy from accessing them. The unresolved issues stored there can go back years, even decades, and may be traumas you have completely forgotten about.

When you realize you feel no connection to your Grounding cord, thank this realization, and continue the practice of Conscious Grounding. Not feeling it can be a good thing. Keep your attention focused on the visualized cord. See the gravity working its ways.

As these begin to clear, your body will feel lighter, happier, and you will start feeling more and more flavors of your own energies. You will get an opportunity to rediscover yourself anew, in a way you were before those traumas and stuck energies lodged in and blocked your energetic access to your own body.

P.S.

Finding sitting meditation challenging? Join me on my podcast where I share "grounding in motion"
www.mahalo.care/podcast/

Khalil Gibran
The Prophet:
On Self-Knowledge

And a man said, Speak to us of Self-Knowledge.
And he answered, saying:
Your hearts know in silence the secrets of the days and
        the nights.
But your ears thirst for the sound of your heart's
        knowledge.
You would know in words that which you have
        always known in thought.
You would touch with your fingers the naked body of
        your dreams.

And it is well you should.
The hidden well-spring of your soul must needs rise
        and run murmuring to the sea;
And the treasure of your infinite depths would be
        revealed to your eyes.
But let there be no scales to weigh your unknown
        treasure;
And seek not the depths of your knowledge with staff
        or sounding line.
For self is a sea boundless and measureless.

Say not, "I have found the truth," but rather,
     "I have found a truth."
Say not, "I have found the path of the soul." Say rather,
     "I have met the soul walking upon my path."
For the soul walks upon all paths.
The soul walks not upon a line, neither does it grow
     like a reed.
The soul unfolds itself, like a lotus of countless petals.

With grace and gratitude
Merina

Made in the USA
Las Vegas, NV
10 May 2024

89787257R00111